Modern Chinese Paintings

The Reyes Collection in the
Ashmolean Museum, Oxford

Modern Chinese Paintings

The Reyes Collection in the Ashmolean Museum, Oxford

Shelagh Vainker

ASHMOLEAN MUSEUM OXFORD
1996

Catalogue of the collection of modern Chinese paintings presented to the Ashmolean Museum in 1995 in honour of Jose Mauricio and Angelita Trinidad Reyes, to accompany an exhibition held in the Museum's McAlpine Gallery from 24 September until 1 December 1996.

British Library Cataloguing in Publication Data
A catalogue record for this book is available from the British Library

ISBN   1 85444 079 9

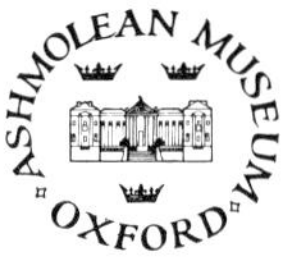

Cover illustration: LIU HAISU *Landscape*
Catalogue number 52

Designed and set in Monotype Bembo by Behram Kapadia
Printed and bound in Singapore by Craft Print PTE Ltd., 1996

ACKNOWLEDGEMENTS

In December 1995 a collection of 130 modern Chinese paintings was generously presented to the Ashmolean Museum in honour of Jose Mauricio and Angelita Trinidad Reyes. This gift forms the largest single benefaction to the Department of Eastern Art since its foundation in 1960, and added to the collection of modern paintings begun by the first Keeper and built up subsequently over many years by Mary Tregear, establishes the Ashmolean as a significant centre for the study of this field of Chinese art.

The present book follows the catalogue presented with the collection, compiled with the assistance of Robert Ribeiro QC, Susan Ribeiro, Thomas Au, Richard Khaw, Ku Wai Sang and Gladys Lo. I should like to express particular thanks to Robert and Susan Ribeiro for their continued interest in the Reyes Collection. The inclusion of the painting inscriptions in original Chinese has been made possible by a grant from the Universities' China Committee in London and I am grateful to Zhang Hongxing for undertaking the task of transcribing the inscriptions. I am also indebted to Professor Glen Dudbridge and Miss Dee Zhang of the Institute of Chinese Studies, Oxford, for generating an accurate Chinese character text. For reasons of space it has not always been possible to include a full transcription, and the translations are provided for non-readers of Chinese. I am grateful to Dr. Anne Farrer of the Department of Oriental Antiquities, British Museum, for her comments on the catalogue entries. Any remaining errors and omissions are my own.

I am grateful to the Ashmolean Museum Photographic Service for their promptness in photographing the collection, and to Wendy Maine for the map which appears on p. 6. The transfer of the collection from Hong Kong to Oxford was generously assisted by Eskenazi Ltd, and the installation of the paintings has been overseen by Mr. David Armitage of the Department of Eastern Art.

Shelagh Vainker

ASSISTANT KEEPER
DEPARTMENT OF EASTERN ART

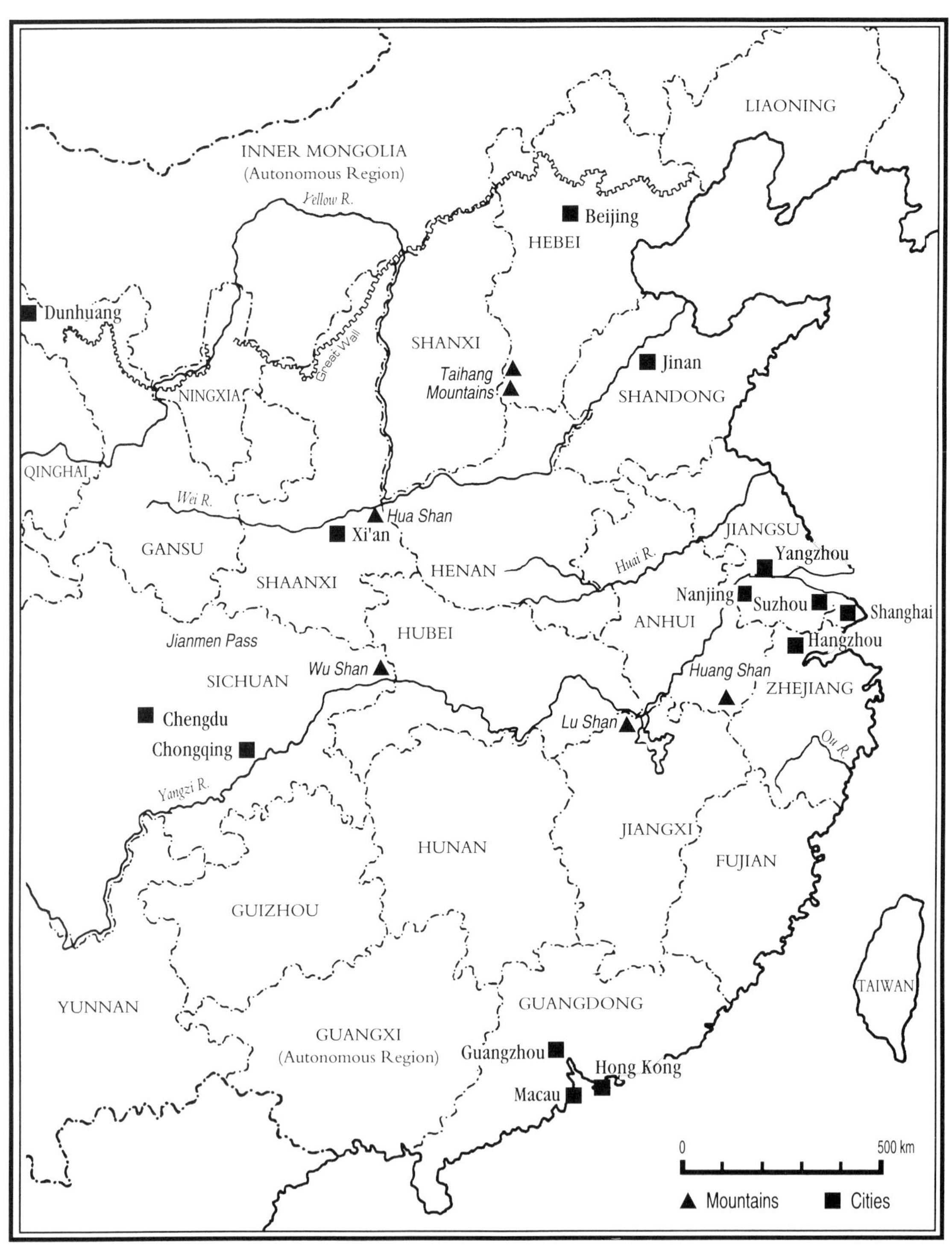

LIAONING
INNER MONGOLIA
(Autonomous Region)
Yellow R.
Beijing
HEBEI
Dunhuang
Great Wall
SHANXI
Jinan
Taihang
Mountains
SHANDONG
NINGXIA
QINGHAI
Wei R.
Hua Shan
Huai R.
JIANGSU
Xi'an
Yangzhou
GANSU
HENAN
Nanjing
Suzhou
Shanghai
SHAANXI
ANHUI
Hangzhou
HUBEI
Huang Shan
Jianmen Pass
Wu Shan
ZHEJIANG
SICHUAN
Lu Shan
Ou R.
Chengdu
Chongqing
Yangzi R.
JIANGXI
HUNAN
FUJIAN
GUIZHOU
YUNNAN
TAIWAN
GUANGDONG
GUANGXI
(Autonomous Region)
Guangzhou
Hong Kong
Macau
0   500 km
Mountains   Cities

INTRODUCTION

The Reyes Collection of modern Chinese paintings covers the period from the middle of the 19th century until late 1995 when the collection was presented to the Ashmolean Museum. Artistically this period includes paintings strictly in the classical tradition and paintings which seek to update that tradition, as well as works embodying a response to Japanese or to Western art and works which reflect international art movements of the late 20th century. Politically it is a period that began under the Qing dynasty, which witnessed the founding of the Republic in 1911 and the establishment in 1949 of the People's Republic of China; it was also a period punctuated by unrest in the form of widescale rebellion, the Sino-Japanese (1937–45) war, civil war and, most recently, the Cultural Revolution (1966–76). A further challenge to politicians, intellectuals and artists alike over the last century-and-a-half has been that of how to respond to the West, and this dilemma has added to the complexity of the history of modern Chinese painting. The plurality of artistic styles that arose in these circumstances, together with the ongoing tension between China's illustrious past and international present, has precluded the decisive formulation of a mainstream in Chinese painting; the Reyes collection, in representing the conservative as well as the innovative painters of each generation, is in keeping with most major collections, public or private, in this field.

The classical artistic tradition which endured so much upheaval originated in the 11th century during the Northern Song (966–1127) dynasty, when the art of calligraphy flourished and the theory and practice of landscape painting developed. The greatest calligraphers of the period – Cai Xiang (1012–67), Su Dongpo (1037–1101), Huang Tingjian (1045–1105) and Mi Fu (1052–1107) – were also writers and officials, and the association of calligraphy with a high degree of formal education in fact persisted from its inception as an art form in the 4th century right up until the 20th century (47). The severely controlled use of the brush for even the most expressive calligraphy provided the basis for painting landscapes in essentially calligraphic style; ink, with the addition of only a very little colour, was brushed onto paper not just to convey the qualities of the writer, but also to construct monumental landscapes which might embody a philosophical view of nature and man's place in the universe, or possibly his own responses to those. The closeness of painting to calligraphy is the reason why signatures on Chinese works of art may be preceded by the character for "written", "drawn", or "painted", used almost interchangeably.

This calligraphic method contrasted sharply with the linear style of both landscape and figure painting in the preceding Tang (618–906) dynasty, when mineral colours and silk, rather than the more responsive paper, had been the standard media. The latter style remained evident however in the Northern Song Imperial Painting Academy, where the use of outline and colour on silk, particularly to produce bird and flower paintings, formed the origins of what is known as decorative painting style. Thus were established the two principal styles of "traditional" Chinese painting; while the decorative survived into modern times (8, 111) there is no doubt that calligraphic painting, almost exclusively landscape, has always in China been highly regarded as the principal form of serious painting. It is known as *wenrenhua*, "literati painting", the work of scholars and officials exchanged as gifts or for favours, as opposed to the "professional" painting produced for sale. The precision of such a distinction between one style and practice and another is of course open to scrutiny, but historically the difference between the literati and the professionals has been expressed, repeatedly. In the 20th century, paintings continuing the *wenren* literati tradition are known as *guohua* or "national painting" and these form the nucleus of the Reyes Collection, as indeed also of the Ashmolean's earlier collection of modern paintings.

LANDSCAPE AND LITERATURE

Landscape subjects may have developed partly as a vehicle for depicting broader thoughts, but their prominence in the classical tradition has been continually reinforced by the reality of China's mountains and rivers. China is a vast country, incorporating mountainous and desert regions as well as fertile plains (45, 69) and tropical areas. Certain mountains have acquired historical associations (9) and religious significance and throughout centuries artists have added to their fame by visiting these imposing sites, and subsequently painting them. Huangshan (Mount Huang) in Anhui province (39, 52, 55, 81) is perhaps the most renowned for dramatic scenery while Lushan in Jiangxi (82), though not a religious site, is famous for the poems as well as the paintings it has inspired. The influence of landscape on painters however goes beyond the depiction of famous places and rivers (42, 68); the empty backgrounds in the animal paintings of Wu Zuoren (93) for example, particularly his camels and yaks, appear only after his visit to Dunhuang, where the vast expanse of the Gobi desert changed his perceptions of space and distance.

Dunhuang is an influential site in the history of Chinese painting. Now a small oasis town in Gansu province in the northwest of China, in the Tang (618–906) dynasty it was a major trading city on the Silk Route, at the point where the road from the Tang capital divided north and south of the Taklamakan desert; the nearby Mogao cave temples are one of the principal Buddhist sites in China. Excavated and enlarged from the 4th century to the 13th, it was in the Tang dynasty that they flourished, and the murals and painted ceilings in colourful linear style form the largest surviving group of Tang painting. The site was largely neglected until early in the 20th century, when it was discovered by foreign archaeologists and explorers, and throughout this century numerous artists have travelled there to see the paintings. Zhang Daqian in particular was impressed by the sculpture and murals of Dunhuang, spending the two years following his 1942 visit producing several hundred figure and landscape paintings copied from or inspired by the cave paintings (113, 116).

The Tang dynasty, and especially the first half of the 8th century, was a period of great achievement in all aspects of Chinese arts and literature, and many of these have been evident in the paintings of subsequent dynasties. Figure paintings in particular have been indebted to Tang style, while subjects taken from Tang history (62) and popular literature (13, 104, 105 A & B) remain current in the late 20th century. Poetry has been even more influential; couplets (21) or whole poems are often inscribed on paintings which may themselves illustrate a famous poem (62), and many more verses, if not actually transcriptions of Tang poems, follow the twenty-eight character format of four seven-syllable lines established in that period. The poetry and calligraphy of the Song (960–1279) dynasty likewise remain prominent in inscriptions and subject matter, even on works which are not obviously in the classical tradition. These tend to refer to painting methods (80, 91, 122) and calligraphic style (74, 107) rather than the historical incidents and figures favoured in the Tang period.

The presence of China's literary and historical past in the paintings of the modern period is thus by no means limited to works which adhere strictly to the tenets of literati painting; the latter are the clearest manifestations of an ancient and apparently almost inescapable past which is implicit in the brushwork and subject matter even of some recent paintings (123, 124), and explicit in the inscriptions of many more (34).

THE LITERATI TRADITION AFTER 1800

The painting style prevalent at the beginning of the 19th century was a conservative continuation of the classical tradition, deriving ultimately from the literati painting of the Song and Yuan (1279–1368) dynasties. The vigour of that tradition had by the 16th century begun to wane, prompting the painter and theorist Dong Qichang (1555–1636), in a grand survey of all previous Chinese painting masterpieces, to state methods not only for appreciating landscapes but also for creating them; he also drew a clear distinction between types of painting that might be regarded as cultivated and types which must be considered vulgar. Dong Qichang's theories were so compelling that few subsequent historians of Chinese painting have escaped their influence, even into modern times.

Those 17th century painters who followed his theories have become known as the Orthodox School, and its principal exponents were Wang Shimin (1592–1680), Wang Jian (1598–1652), Wang Hui (1632–1717), Wang Yuanqi (1642–1715), Wu Li (1632–1718) and Yun Shouping (1633–90). Throughout the 19th century there were many painters who worked in the disciplined techniques of the Orthodox School, regarding themselves explicitly as part of a lineage that extended through Wang Shimin or Wang Hui to the Yuan masters and their Song predecessors. Such painters, particularly earlier in the 19th century but also later, learnt calligraphy and painting from private tutors and family collections, or collections to which they had access through family connections. In conjunction with a classical education, such training equipped a young artist for employment in government and the life of a scholar-official, or literatus.

Beijing (Peking), as the capital city and centre of government, was a prominent literary and artistic centre throughout the Qing (1644–1911) dynasty, attracting artists from the provinces in addition to the groups of painters already associated with the court. The latter dwindled in number throughout the turbulant years of the 19th century, yet it was in Beijing that the most conservative artists of the early 20th century established their painting associations. Foremost amongst these was the Hu She association founded by Jin Cheng (1878–1926), dedicated to the perpetuation of literati painting through imitation of Song and Yuan masters. Artists active in various other associations included Chen Shaomei (1909–54) (5, 6), Yu Fei'an (1889–1959) (111), Xiao Sun (1883–1944) (94) and Chen Hengke (1876–1923) (3, 4). Chen Hengke, though from a Jiangxi literati family, was not as intensely traditional as some other artists; he was interested in the 17th century Individualist painters rather than their Orthodox contemporaries and helped establish the career of Qi Baishi (1863–1957), who nowadays is usually associated with the Shanghai School. Shanghai, opened as a treaty port in 1842, was in the 19th century a centre of innovative painting, but also attracted literati painters (see below) including Wu Guxiang (1848–1903) (88) and later the prominent connoisseur and collector Wu Hufan (1894–1968) (89, 90).

THE SHANGHAI SCHOOL

The term "Shanghai School" is used to denote a group of artists whose connections with that city vary from native to tenuous, but whose paintings and working methods share a common break with established early 19th century painting style.

The early Qing Individualists who dissented from the art historical theory of painting propounded by Dong Qichang sought instead to recapture the essence of Song painting by responding to nature directly, and the most influential of these was to be Shi Tao (1642–1707), also known as Dao Ji. This personal method was taken up in the 18th century by painters associated with the city of Yangzhou, and it is these artists whose circumstances and paintings may be compared to those of the Shanghai School.

Yangzhou, on the north bank of the Yangzi, was a flourishing port as early as the Tang dynasty and in the 18th century it prospered again, as a centre of the salt trade. Its rich merchant population, keen to patronise artists but often lacking education in painting and calligraphy, were receptive to unconventional styles and content to buy direct. These precedents were developed further in Shanghai, a city founded on trade and which moreover accommodated by the mid-19th century a wide mix of nationalities and social classes. In addition to Chinese and foreign merchants and entrepreneurs, Shanghai's population included refugees from the Taiping Rebellion which raged across east China during the 1850s. The mild, fertile eastern provinces of Jiangsu and Zhejiang have brought forth the most elegant and erudite scholars of most eras of Chinese history; those migrating to late Qing Shanghai thus included traditional painters seeking safety from unrest as well as painters from an even wider geographical area attracted by the commercial possibilities of the most prosperous and cosmopolitan of the new treaty ports.

The earlier painters associated with the Shanghai School include Zhao Zhiqian (1829–84), Ren Xiong (1820–57) (72) and Xu Gu (1823–96) (102, 103). Zhao

Zhiqian came from a literati family in Zhejiang, Ren Xiong was an artist from the Shanghai area and Xu Gu belonged to a military family from Yangzhou, providing a link between the Eccentric painters and their artistic heirs. Xu Gu is known for a reserved painting style and while his subjects – squirrels, goldfish, plants, vegetables – all have antecedents as far back in some cases as Song court painting, his handling of them in large formats and a combination of dry and loose brushwork represents a new departure. Ren Yi (1840–95) (73), the leading artist in late 19th century Shanghai, is renowned for enlarging the subject repertoire, painting heroes from popular literature and legend, often in exaggerated or distorted style, in addition to traditional bird and plant subjects. Such breaking of the boundaries between decorative and literati subjects and brushwork, and their re-configuration to embrace painting forms previously considered vulgar, form the principal contribution of the so-called Shanghai School to the development of modern Chinese painting. The widespread sale of paintings within Shanghai was also at odds with literati practice and Ren Yi, who enjoyed great commercial success, was as well-known for the wealth he accumulated as for the paintings from which it derived. His pupil Wu Changshuo (1844–1927), as a highly trained painter and calligrapher with a particular interest in seal-carving, succeeded in tempering the low regard in which Ren and others were held; he also carried forward the new style to another generation of painters.

MODERNIZATION 1900–1949

The first half of the 20th century was a period in which approaches to painting underwent great change. Not only had the events of the 19th century weakened the role of traditionalism, but the circumstances in which artists worked and paintings became known broadened enormously.

Publishing houses, in Shanghai particularly, began producing magazines and journals in the early years of the century; pictorial publications increased steadily and in the 1930s paintings were regularly reproduced in newspapers. Previously, calligraphy and paintings had been accessible only to those who owned them and their acquaintances, and were reproducible only in the principally monochrome forms of stone rubbings or woodcuts. Photographic reproduction made it possible for people from all levels of society to develop an interest in the subject, and this popularization was reinforced by the introduction of the art exhibition. Before the 20th century, paintings were not displayed in public, but viewed privately by groups of collectors, and there were no museums or art galleries. The first exhibitions were held in the British and French concessions in Shanghai, and in the second decade of the century exhibitions of contemporary paintings were held in Beijing as well. New artists seeking sales, who in the past had only been able to leave their work at mounting shops, now submitted it for exhibition and although the paintings might not be viewed by large crowds, they probably would be reviewed in magazines and newspapers.

New opportunities for artistic training also arose in this period. The first art school in China was opened in 1912 in Shanghai by Liu Haisu; Liu was sixteen years old at the time and the school consisted of perhaps a dozen members, but within ten years had several hundred students. At around the same time several universities set up art departments, so that the study of painting became a possibility for all students able to contemplate a university education.

Art publishing, education and exhibitions were not confined to Shanghai for in the treaty port of Canton, all these activities were initiated by Gao Jianfu (1879–1951) (22). Gao had at the turn of the century studied in Japan, where he encountered both the movement to revitalize Japanese painting through synthesis with Western models, and the Chinese revolutionary Sun Yat-Sen, with whose political movement he became involved. After the Revolution of 1911 Gao Jianfu, his brother Gao Qifeng (1889–1933) and Chen Shuren (1883–1948) founded a movement called "New National Painting", which sought not only to invigorate traditional painting through the introduction of chiaroscuro, perspective and other Western watercolour techniques, but also to modernize it by depicting symbols of modern technology in their landscapes. The movement, based in Canton, became known as the Lingnan School (22, 27, 48, 119, 120, 130), and remains active.

Gao Jianfu was amongst the earliest of many Chinese painters to study in Japan. Others went to Europe, so that by the third decade of the 20th century the influence on Chinese painting may be said to have been truly international. Foreign influence became in part institutionalized by the invitations extended to many returned students to head art academies and university art departments. Three prominent European-trained artists all of whom studied at the Ecole des Beaux-Arts in Paris were Xu Beihong (1898–1953) (98, 99, 100, 101), Lin Fengmian (1900–91) (49, 50, 51), and Liu Haisu (1896–1994) (52). Unsurprisingly, each took up a different aspect of European painting, and assimilated Western style into their works to varying extents. Xu Beihong was impressed with Academic Realism and spent much time with Dagnan-Bouveret. He worked hard at life drawing, and on his return to China produced several large scale didactic oil paintings in the manner of grand historical painting in Europe. Lin Fengmian was sympathetic to the view of the early Republican intellectual leader Cai Yuanpei that art should replace religion, and he was attracted to the epic qualities of Renaissance art; in his own paintings however, the colours and structures of Matisse, the Fauves and the Parisian avant-garde are to the fore. His works are the most colourful of all 20th century Chinese paintings, yet he often retains elements of traditional composition. Liu Haisu preferred Cézanne and Van Gogh, and indeed for many years worked principally in oils rather than the Chinese medium. When he did address traditional painting, he assimilated his understanding of oil painting and colours to great effect. A painter who was similarly successful in absorbing Western colour techniques into traditional painting, though he never studied in Europe, was Zhu Qizhan (125, 126).

Liu Haisu returned to teach in Shanghai, while Lin Fengmian was appointed head of the new National Art Academy in Hangzhou, Zhejiang province and Xu Beihong was given posts in Shanghai and subsequently Nanjing and Beijing. Their different theories of how to reform Chinese painting, and the fact that students in art academies were now exposed to many teachers and styles of painting, rather than a single tutor, vastly increased the possibilities for artistic renewal.

During the upheavals of the decade 1928–37, Nanjing became the seat of the

Nationalist Government. The Lingnan School, unaffected, continued to evolve its own criteria for painting while many of the conservative traditionalists in Beijing remained there. These included Pu Xinyu (1896–1963) (63, 64, 65), a member of the Qing Imperial family who finally moved in the late 1940s to Taiwan where he became the leading classical painter. Nanjing became an important centre for painting, with the art department of National Central University headed by Fu Baoshi (1904–65) (17–21), recently returned from studying in Japan and who, after Huang Binhong (1864–1955) (29, 30), is the leading literati painter of this century.

At the onset of the Sino-Japanese war in 1937 the University, along with numerous other institutions and professional individuals, moved to west China and was based at Chongqing in Sichuan province. For the following eight years there was a concentration of painters in Sichuan, including Lin Fengmian, Ding Yanyong, Xu Beihong, Fu Baoshi and Zhang Daqian, and numerous exhibitions were held (98). The dramatic scenery of Sichuan may have impressed some artists (20) while others took the opportunity to travel from Sichuan to other areas of western China (100, 113, 116) but on the whole, the painters appear to have developed the styles they were already practising rather than being profoundly influenced by local conditions.

Those artists who were more politically involved, in the anti-Japanese campaign and the Communist struggle, travelled the country during this period, painting war pictures and producing propaganda. Much of this took the form of woodcuts, both because this was the medium of Käthe Kollwitz and other international socialist artists first introduced to China by the novelist and reformer Lu Xun, and because it related to New Year prints, the only form of pictorial art familiar to the illiterate country-dwellers whose support the socialists were seeking to enlist. These artists included Shi Lu (78, 79) and Li Keran (43–47), both of whom were to be involved in the development of painting practices after the establishment of the People's Republic of China.

PAINTING IN THE PEOPLE'S REPUBLIC OF CHINA, 1949–

When the Communists established the People's Republic of China in October 1949, they regarded the work of artists as approaching that of writers in its potential to affect people's thoughts. The educational opportunities, artistic choices and economic freedom that had become available to Chinese painters in the first half of the 20th century all gradually became subject to government control, and it was increasingly difficult for a painter to sell his work. By the mid-1950s most artists, like everyone else, were employed by the state for a fixed wage and their work belonged to the state. Art schools were directed only to teach officially sanctioned styles, thereby controlling each new generation of artists. Established painters could only function through state-run agencies, the local, regional and national artists associations run by the carefully vetted members themselves in accordance with political directives from ultimately, the government.

The ideology that drove these reforms was Mao's view, stated at the Yan'an Forum on Art and Literature in 1942, that art should serve the masses; writers and artists should be spokesmen for the masses and also educators of the masses, in effect by presenting to them that which had been determined by the Communist Party on their behalf. The fact that most artists worked in Western media or the traditional Chinese mode presented a problem of style; Western painting was feudal in origin while traditional Chinese style carried the stigma of the privilege associated with literati painting. The solutions included work inspired by Soviet socialist realist painting, and pictures based on New Year prints and other folk art. The extent to which the individualism of literati or Western style painting was in fact tolerated varied throughout the 1950s, and although some painters were assigned to produce commercial art, there certainly did appear paintings which were not obviously distinguishable from works of the previous decade (111).

In 1956 came the Hundred Flowers campaign, named after Confucius' saying "Let a hundred flowers bloom and a hundred schools of thought contend", promising an unprecedented degree of artistic freedom and which has been viewed both as part of a longer-running attempt to carry intellectuals with the Party rather than resort to overt censorship, and as a ploy to reveal disloyalty to the Party. In 1958 this freedom was curtailed by the Anti-Rightist campaign, the first of a succession of campaigns in which intellectuals might be branded enemies of the state, and the beginning of a period of great suffering for many artists. Painting content and style were subjected to intense political scrutiny, and it was in this period that overt political allusions, such as landscapes dominated by red, began to proliferate in works of art, and yet this period of difficulty during the late 1950s was followed by a few years in the early 1960s when artists once again enjoyed recognition and a certain amount of freedom, and some of the most sensitive *guohua* landscapes of the late 20th century were painted (19).

In 1966 Mao launched the Cultural Revolution. In the ten years that followed, it became almost impossible for artists to work, and little teaching took place. The painting collections, libraries and work of many of the painters represented in this catalogue were destroyed, with the artists in some cases being driven to do this themselves. Though many of them survived, younger painters are now deracinated from the tradition that was already under strain from political events; to the tensions of past and present, Chinese and Western, must be added that between younger and older artists. After 1979, when government control over art was loosened and it became once more possible for artists to sell their work, many younger artists enjoyed the possibility for self-expression by following Western artistic trends, including installation and performance art. The repression which followed the events at Tiananmen Square in 1989 eventually gave rise to movements such as Political Pop and Cynical Realism (128). There is once again an art market in China, and painters increasingly sell their work in Hong Kong and throughout the Far East, Europe and America as well. Some paintings are geared to those markets but, just as conservative and innovative styles existed together in an earlier period, it is true that within China today, unexposed, ink paintings and calligraphy continue to be exchanged amongst friends.

THE CATALOGUE

1 BAO CHENCHU 包辰初

1928–

Landscape

INK AND COLOUR ON PAPER
HANGING SCROLL, FRAMED, 68.6 × 45.6 CM
EA 1995.167
Signed 辰初 *Chenchu*

Bao Chenchu is a *guohua* landscape painter from Longyou, Zhejiang province. The composition of a long view across water and spits of land is a traditional one, occurring particularly on paintings in handscroll format. The buff, green and blue-grey washes use the colours of classical landscape while the large bright *dian* are distinctly modern, and typical of Bao Chenchu's more recent work.

2 BAO CHENCHU 包辰初

1928–

Landscape

INK AND COLOUR ON PAPER
SQUARE PAINTING IN CHINESE MOUNT,
FRAMED, 82 × 82 CM
EA 1995.168
Signed 辰初 *Chenchu*

Modern aspects of traditional landscape painting include the introduction of substantial colour and simplification of composition. This painting displays both, though the dominating bright orange is unusual even in contemporary works, and there is little structure to the landscape.

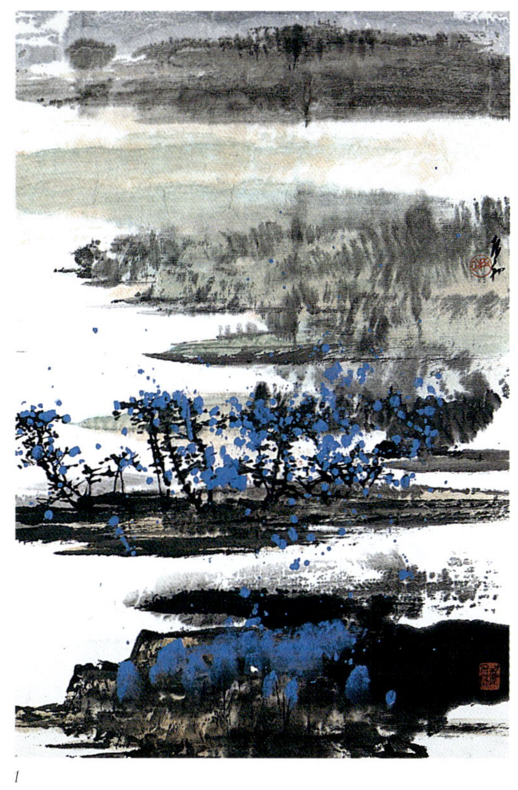

1

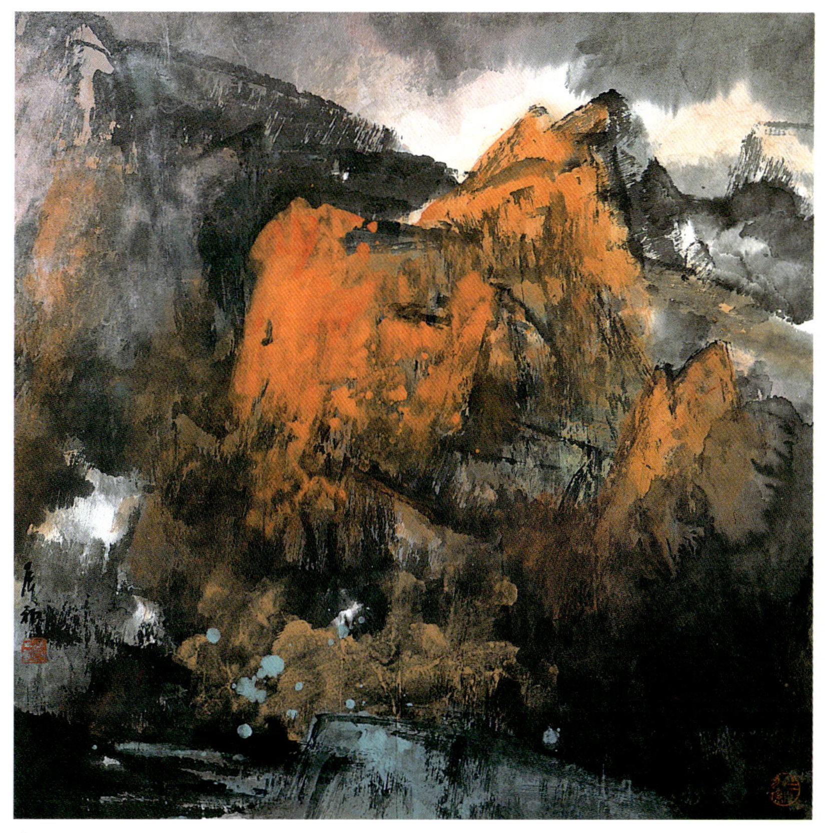

2

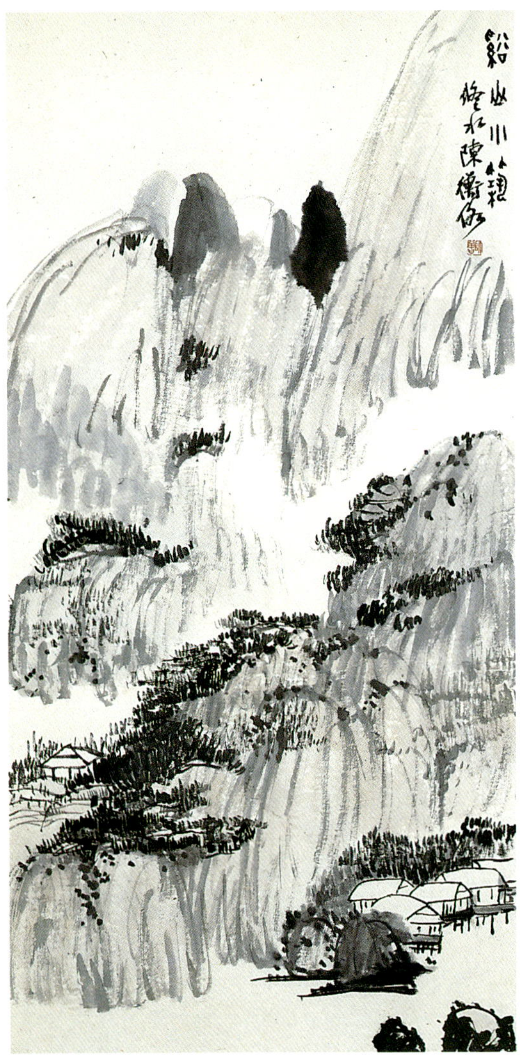

3

3   CHEN HENGKE 陳衡恪
1876–1923

Landscape

INK AND SLIGHT COLOUR ON PAPER

HANGING SCROLL, FRAMED, 119.5 × 60 CM

EA 1995.169

Inscribed: 溪山小築　修水陳衡恪
*Buildings amidst streams and mountains, Xiushui
Chen Hengke*

Though one of the founders of the conservative
art association which dominated Beijing painting
circles in the early twentieth century, Chen Hengke
from Xiushui in Jiangxi province is known as an
innovative artist. His modern outlook, and his
experience of foreign painting styles while in Japan,
are evident in the loose brushwork and rapid
execution of this relatively free composition.

4   CHEN HENGKE 陳衡恪
1876–1923

Calligraphy

INK ON PAPER

PAIR OF HANGING SCROLLS, FRAMED, EACH
130 × 30.9 CM

EA 1995.170 a,b

Signed　陳衡恪　　*Chen Hengke*

Chen Hengke began his career as a pupil of Wu
Changshuo (1844–1927), a painter renowned
for his interest in ancient calligraphic styles. The
present calligraphy, in the style of oracle bone script
of the Shang (c.1600–c.1050 BC) dynasty, is
possibly inspired by his teacher.

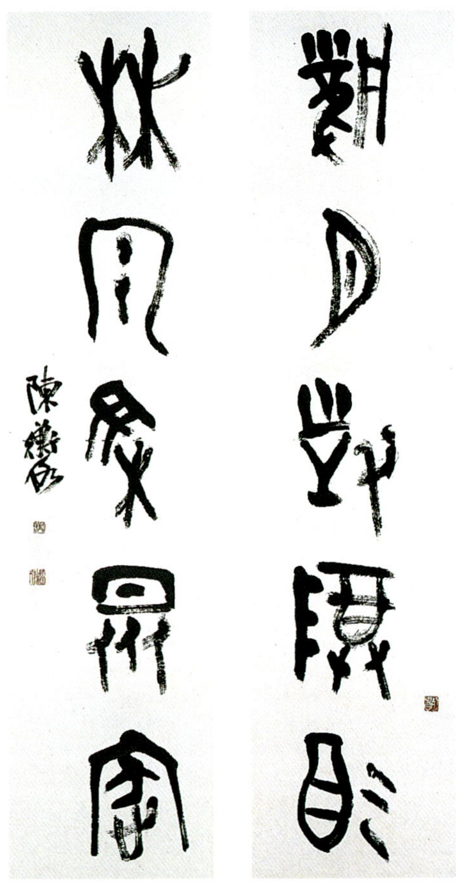

4 *left*   4 *right*

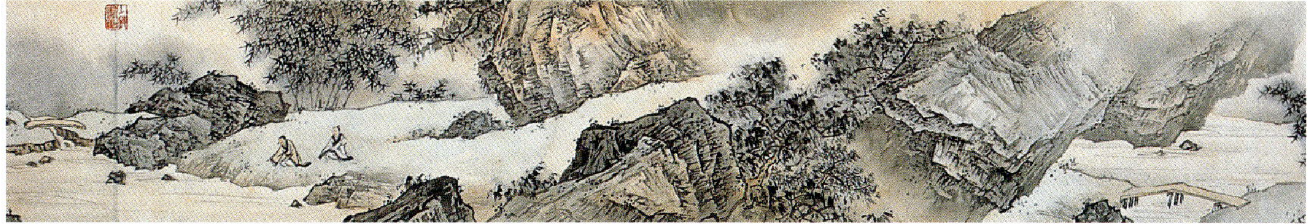

5 (detail)

5   CHEN SHAOMEI 陳少梅
1909–54

Landscape

INK AND COLOUR ON PAPER
HANDSCROLL, 16 × 394 CM, WITH COLOPHON,
16 × 55.5 CM
EA 1995.171
Inscribed:　小石潭紀圖
Inspired by "A Record of the Small Stone Pool"
Signed　少梅陳雲彰　　*Shaomei Chen Yunzhang*

Chen Shaomei was a versatile professional painter
active in Peking at a time when conservative literati
styles prevailed there. This long composition is
painted in the meandering, contemplative mode
suited to the handscroll format and its style, with
colour washes and heavy ink, is that of Southern
Song (1127–1279) academic painting. The
colophon appended to it is written by the artist.
"A Record of the Small Stone Pool" was written
by Liu Zongyuan (AD 773–819).

6   CHEN SHAOMEI 陳少梅
1909–54

Scholar in a landscape

INK AND COLOUR ON PAPER
HANGING SCROLL, 103 × 42.4 CM
EA 1995.172
Inscribed:　春廬寒雨石門泉 遠似虹霓近若煙 獨洗蒼苔
注雲壑 懸飛白鶴繞青田
28-character poem
Signed:　少梅陳雲彰　*Shaomei Chen Yunzhang*

The influence of the leading painters of the
Southern Song (1127–1279) Academy Ma Yuan
and Xia Gui is evident here in the diagonal balance
of the composition, the thick meandering outlines
of the trees and rocks, and the extensive colour wash.

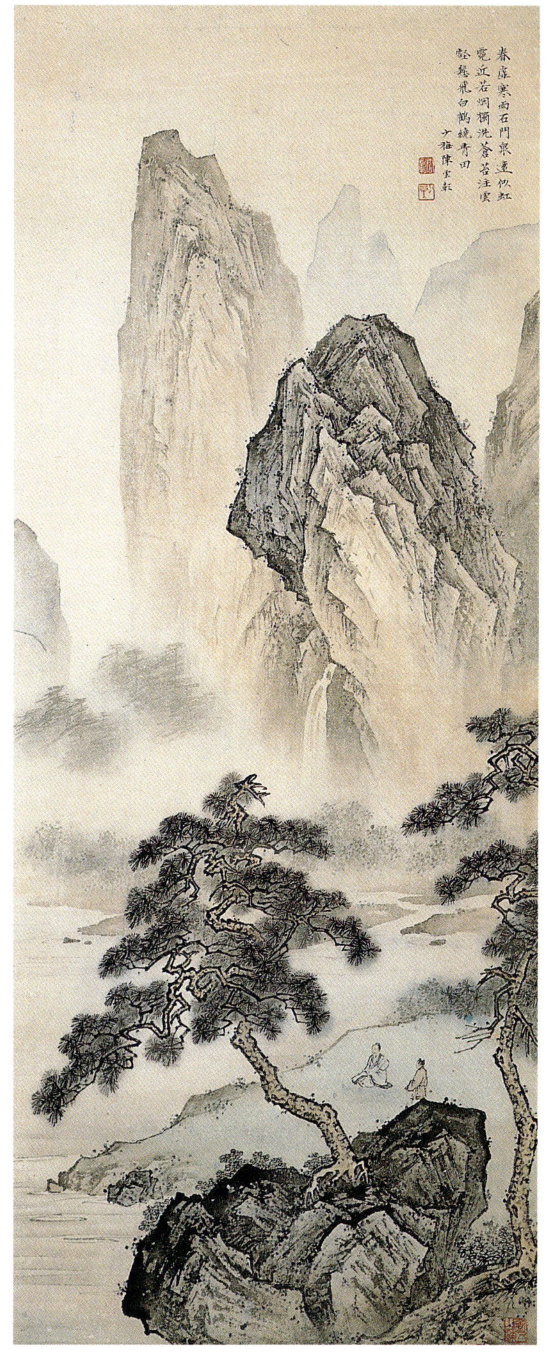

6

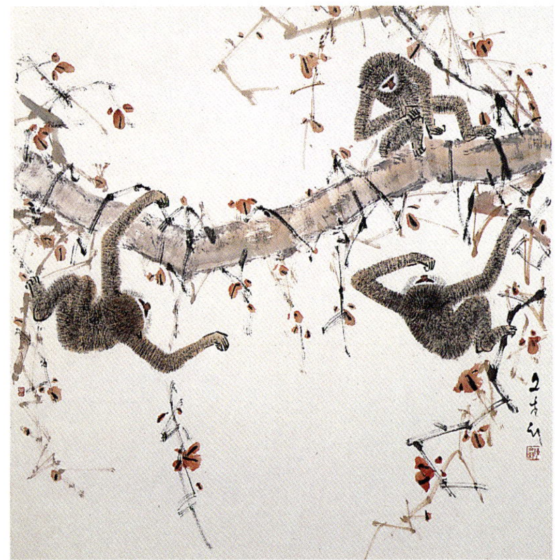

7

7 CHEN WENXI 陳文希
1908–

Gibbons

INK AND COLOUR ON PAPER
HANGING SCROLL, FRAMED, 68.5 × 67.5 CM
EA 1995.297
Signed: 文希作 *Wenxi zuo*

Chen Wenxi is from Guangdong but since the late
1940s has spent much time in Singapore and other
parts of Asia. Most of his works depict animals and
in painting gibbons, a favoured subject, he uses
quite dry ink with a wide, fine-haired brush.

8 CHEN ZHIFO 陳之佛
1896–1962

Bird on a branch

INK AND COLOUR ON PAPER
HANGING SCROLL, 132.5 × 42.8 CM
EA 1995.173
Signed: 陳之佛 *Chen Zhifo*

Early in his career Chen Zhifo was interested in
ornament and design and his paintings, particularly
those produced between 1935 and 1949, are chiefly
in the decorative, meticulous style associated with
Song (960–1279) court painting. The composition
of this painting and the use of opaque pigments
may be compared to porcelain decoration, a subject
on which Chen had previously published, while the
intermingling of colours on the branches is a
modern technique.

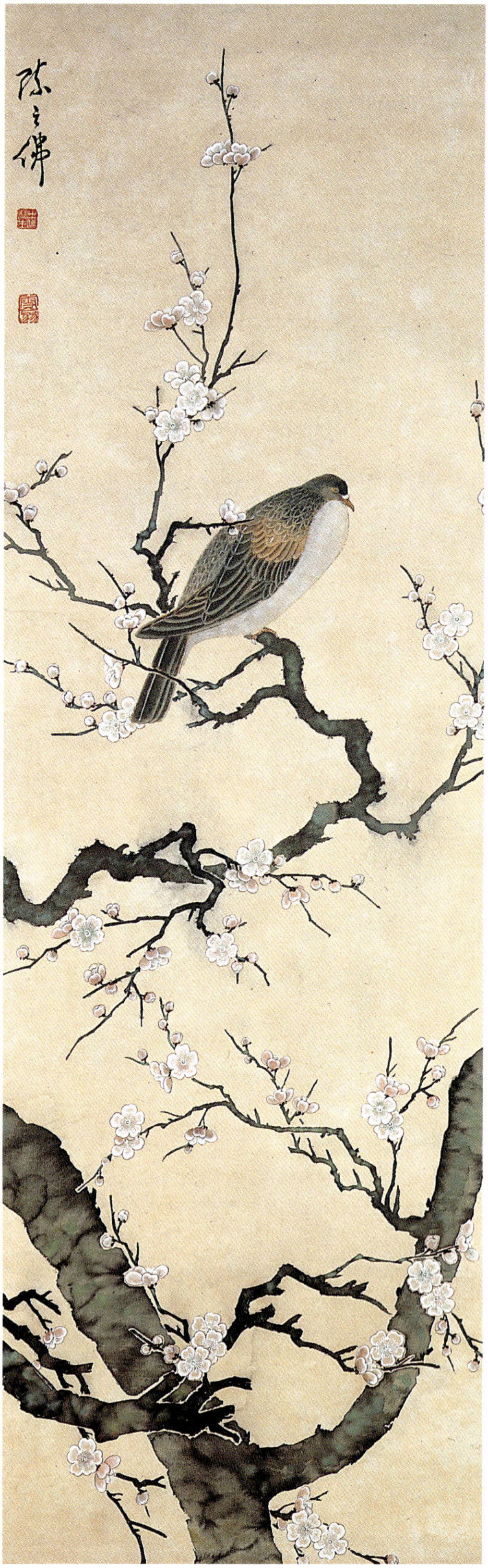

8

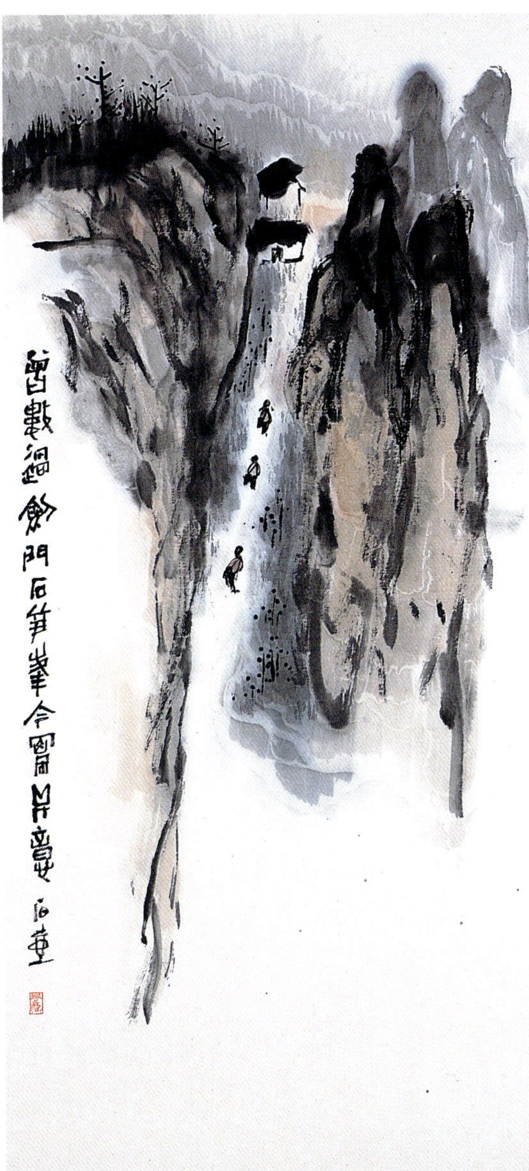

9

9 CHEN ZIZHUANG 陳子莊
1913–76

Landscape with figures

INK AND COLOUR ON PAPER
HANGING SCROLL, FRAMED, 95.5 × 43.9 CM
EA 1995.174

Inscribed: 曾數過劍門石筍　今寫其意石壺
*In the past I have crossed Shisun peak at Jianmen,
today I describe its presence　Shi Hu*

This simple yet uncharacteristically monumental
landscape, signed with the artist's alternative name
Shi Hu, depicts the notoriously treacherous
Jianmen pass in his native Sichuan province. It was
through this pass that the Tang emperor Minghuang
(r.712–56) fled from his capital; the perils of the
landscape are recorded in some of the most famous
Tang dynasty poems and paintings.

10 CHENG SHIFA 程十髮
1921–

Birds, flowers and calligraphy

INK AND COLOUR ON PAPER
ALBUM OF THIRTEEN LEAVES, EACH 34 × 42 CM
APPROX.
EA 1995.175 a–m

1995.175 e (illustrated) inscribed: 程十髮制時戊午仲春
Done (by) Cheng Shifa in Spring 1978

The highly colourful bird and flower paintings are
loosely painted in the traditional mineral and plant
pigments combined with ink favoured by Cheng
Shifa. In the preface to a volume of bird and flower
paintings published around the time this album was
painted, Cheng describes the genre as a supplement
to figure painting, which has always been his
principal concern.

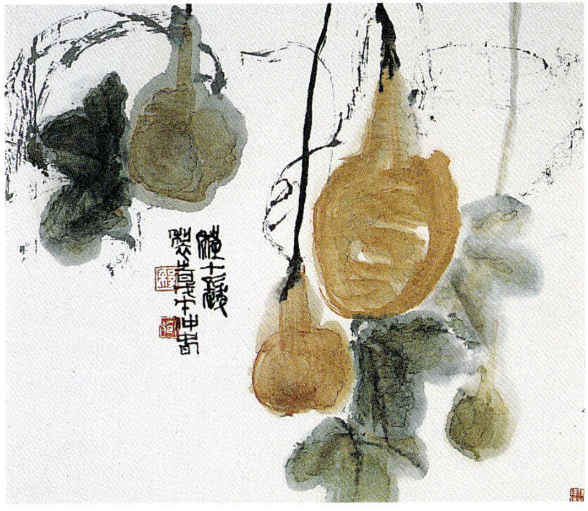

10

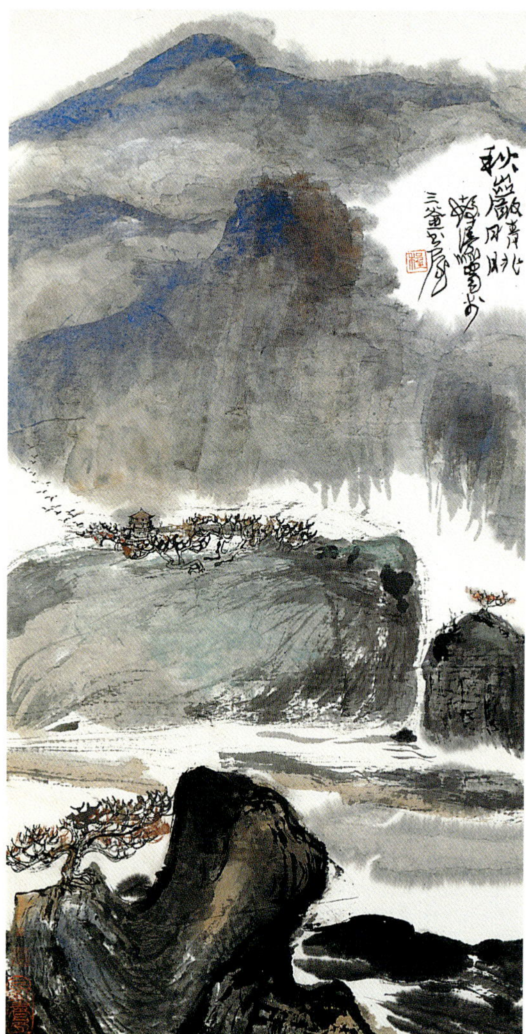

11 CHENG SHIFA 程十髮
1921–

Landscape

INK AND COLOUR ON PAPER

HANGING SCROLL IN WESTERN MOUNT,
FRAMED, 97.5 × 49 CM

EA 1995.178

Inscribed: 秋岩晴眺 十髮漫筆於三釜書屋
*Clear view across autumn cliffs Jotted by Shifa at the
Sanfu studio*

Cheng Shifa was born in Shanghai, where most of
his career has been spent. He practised landscape
painting before taking up illustration and figure
painting, for which he is now better known.
Landscapes such as this are relatively few but the
loose brushwork and the use of colour are typical of
his work.

12 CHENG SHIFA 程十髮
1921–

Lychees and fish

INK AND COLOUR ON PAPER

HANGING SCROLL, FRAMED, 95.5 × 44.3 CM

EA 1995.179

Inscribed: ＿ 衝老兄補壁 十髮寫贈
Painted for Mr. ? Chong, to cover the walls (by) Shifa

The composition of fish depicted beneath over-
hanging branches may be compared with that of
Cui Zifan (see cat. no.14). The inscription, which
is written in characters in archaic style, indicates
that the painting was produced as a commission, or
possibly a gift.

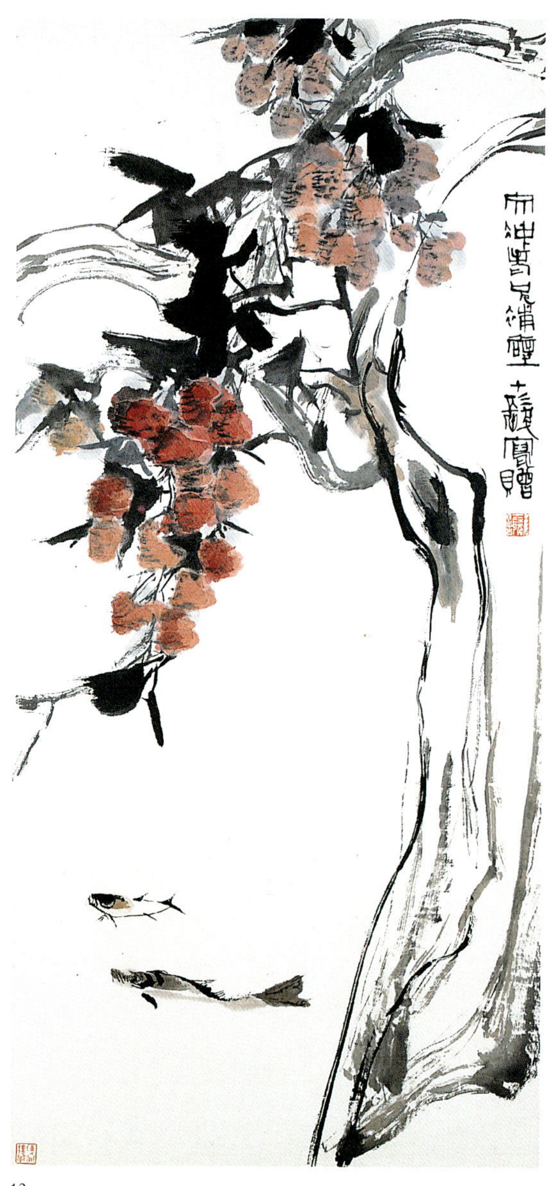

13 CHENG SHIFA 程十髮
1921–

Zhong Kui the Demon Queller

INK AND COLOUR ON PAPER

HANGING SCROLL, FRAMED, 103.2 × 68.5

EA 1995.180

Inscribed: 92-character inscription ending

雲間程十髮 讀沈括補筆談並識於黃浦西岸

Cheng Shifa of Yunjian inspired by Shen Kuo's sequel to the Mengxi bitan, writing on the west bank of the Huangpu

Zhong Kui, associated with upholding righteousness and opposing evil, is a popular figure in Chinese legend and appears in Daoist, Buddhist and folk paintings from as early as the Tang dynasty. Shen Kuo is a famous Northern Song (960–1127) dynasty writer, and one of the first to record the legend of Zhong Kui; the Huangpu River runs through the artist's native city of Shanghai. Cheng Shifa specialised in figure painting and this powerful image is representative of his best work in the genre.

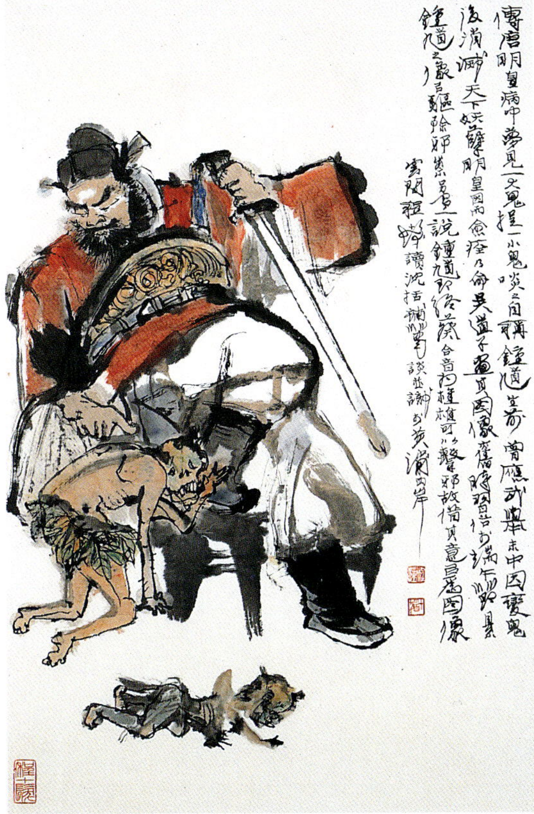

13

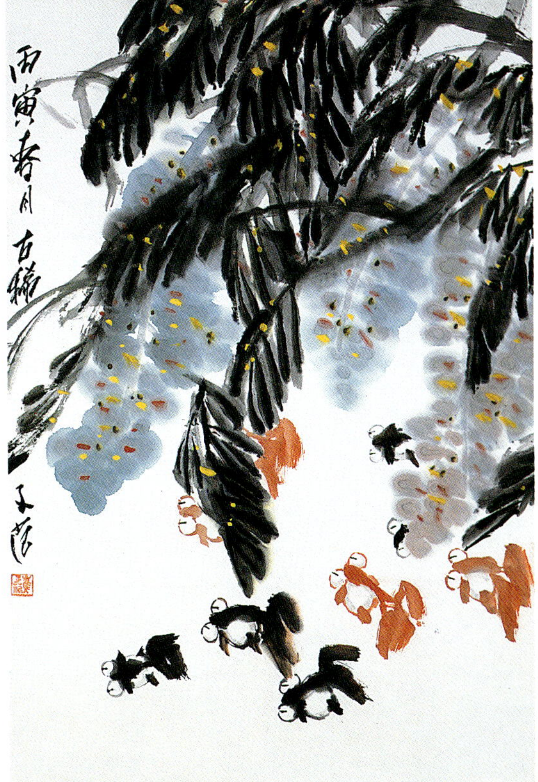

14

14 CUI ZIFAN 崔子範
1915–

Goldfish and wisteria

INK AND COLOUR ON PAPER

HANGING SCROLL, 97 × 66 CM

EA 1995.181

Inscribed: 丙寅春月　子範
Zifan, Spring 1986

Cui Zifan from Shandong province was a pupil of Qi Baishi and after 1956 became a leading member of the Beijing Painting Academy, known for his free brushwork style and use of colour. The pink, turquoise and yellow in this painting bring a contemporary feel to the traditional subject of goldfish, a genre established shortly after they were first bred for ornamental purposes in the eleventh century.

15 DING YANYONG 丁衍庸
1902–78

Birds and fish

INK AND COLOUR ON PAPER

TWO ALBUM LEAVES, MOUNTED AS HANGING
SCROLL, EACH 34.5 × 34.5 CM

EA 1995.182 a,b

Each inscribed: 丁衍庸寫
Drawn by Ding Yanyong

Ding Yanyong studied in Japan while young and for
some years was greatly influenced by the European
paintings he encountered there, particularly those
of Matisse. Though he later renounced Western
style, his use of flat colour with extensive ink is in
neither the Chinese decorative bird and flower
tradition, nor that of ink figure painting. Ducks
painted in this style are a favoured subject of Ding
Yanyong.

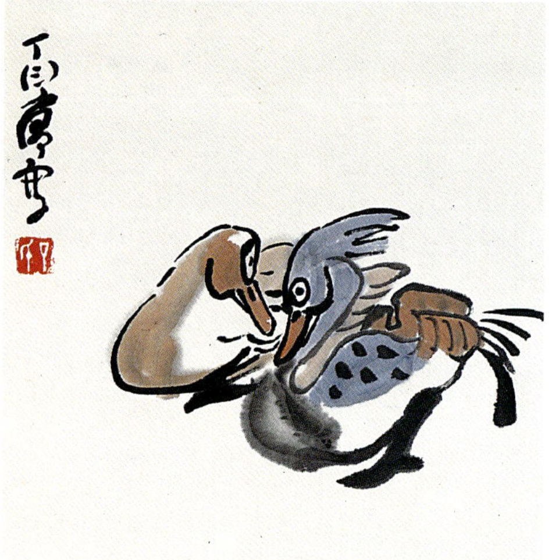

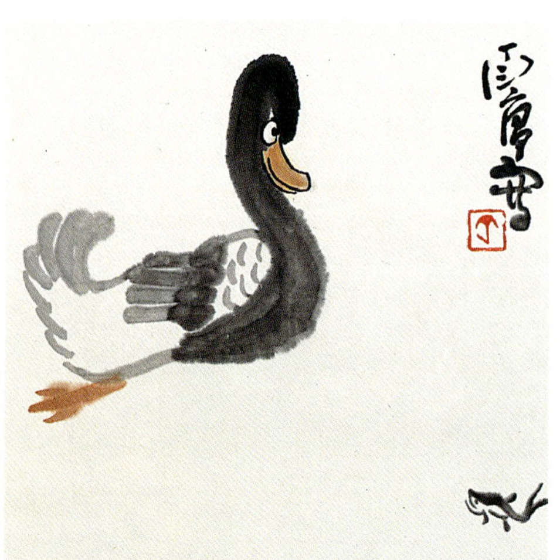

15

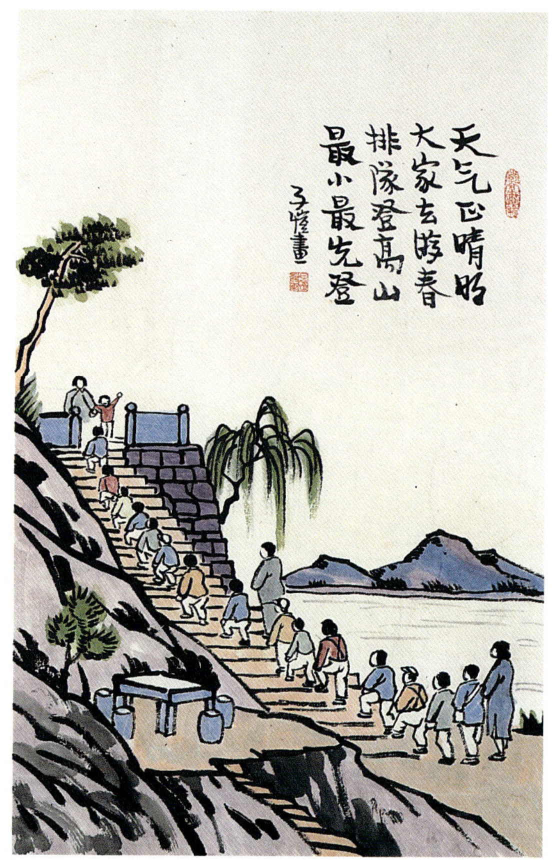

16

16 FENG ZIKAI 豐子愷
1898–1975

Climbing in Spring

INK AND COLOUR ON PAPER

HANGING SCROLL, MOUNTED, 63.2 × 40.5 CM

EA 1995.183

Inscribed: 天氣正晴明大家去游春排隊登高山
最小最先登 子愷畫

*In fine weather everyone goes for a Spring walk,
queuing to climb the tall mountain the smallest climbs
first Painted by Zikai*

Feng Zikai, who is written of both as a Buddhist
and a socialist, is best known as a cartoonist and
illustrator to the works of the early 20th century
novelist and reformer Lu Xun. Much of his work is
therefore in the form of line drawings or woodcut
illustrations; larger paintings in colour, like this, are
relatively few and are thought to date around 1949.

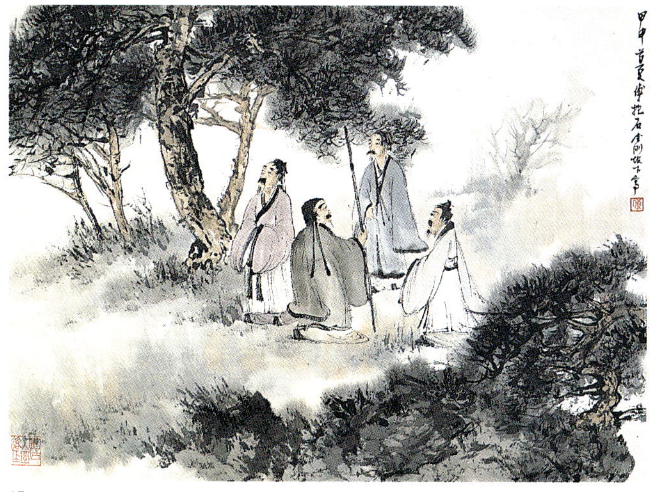

17

17 Attributed to
FU BAOSHI 傅抱石
1904–65

Scholars in a wood

INK AND COLOUR ON PAPER
HANGING SCROLL, 33 × 45.7 CM
EA 1995.184
Inscribed: 甲申首夏傅抱石 金剛坡下寫
Drawn summer 1944 by Fu Baoshi at Jin'gangpo

Fu Baoshi painted many historical figure studies
between 1937 and 1945 while living near Chongqing in Sichuan province. The same group of
figures appears in two paintings dated 1944, now in
Nanjing Museum, one of which bears the title
Along the scenic mountain path.

18 FU BAOSHI 傅抱石
1904–65

Goddess

INK AND COLOUR ON PAPER
HANGING SCROLL, 54 × 45 CM
EA 1995.185
Inscribed: 雲漢同志屬 畫即乞敎正 一九六二年三月抱石
南京幷記
*Painted for Mr. Yun Han, Fu Baoshi, Nanjing, March
1962*

Fu Baoshi painted figures similar to this during the
1940s when his subjects were taken from early
literature, including the Nine Songs of the Eastern
Zhou (771–221 BC) dynasty. One of these depicts
the Lady of the Xiang, daughter of the legendary
Emperor Yao and subject of one of the Nine songs,
while another is a mountain spirit. The style derives
from Tang (618–906) figure painting.

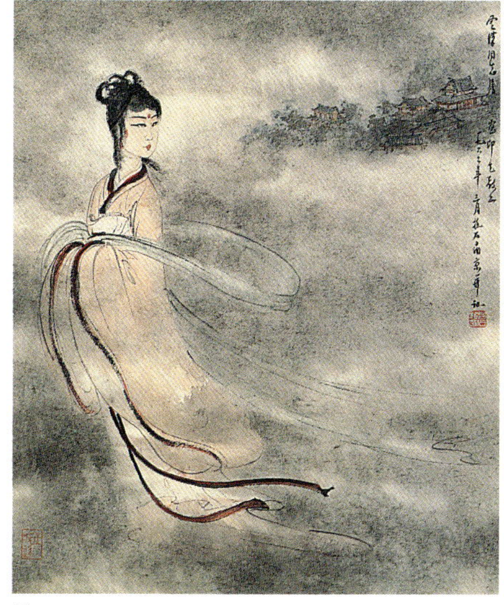

18

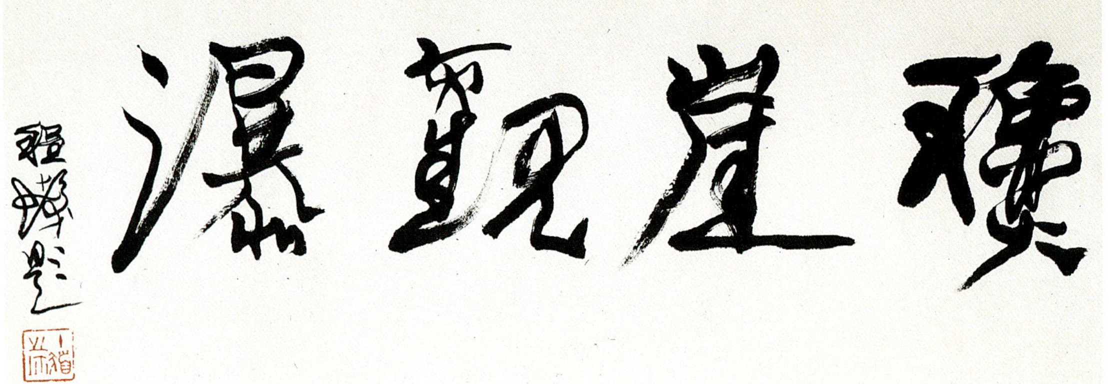

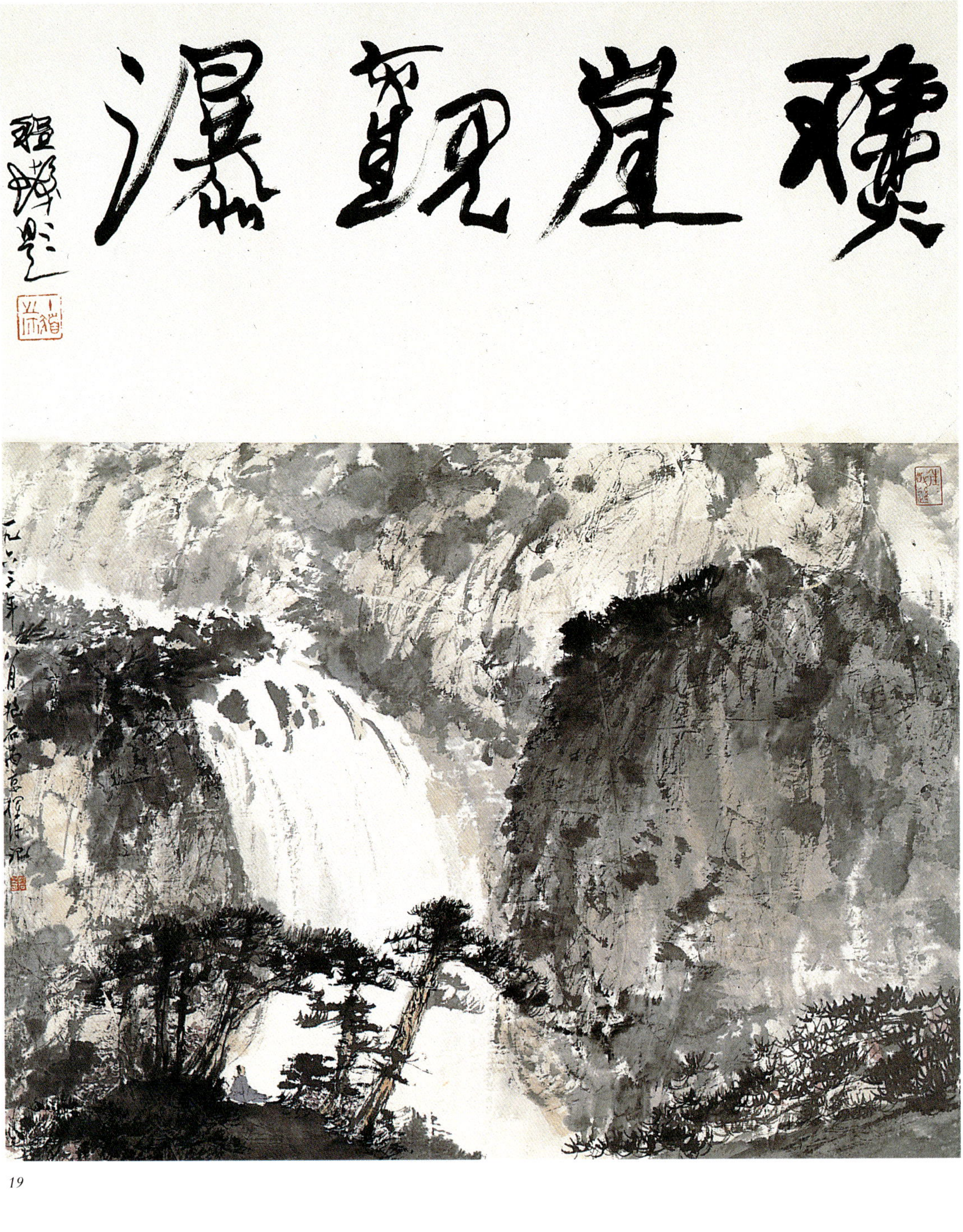

19

19   FU BAOSHI 傅抱石
1904–65

and CHENG SHIFA 程十髮
1921–

Landscape and calligraphy

INK AND SLIGHT COLOUR AND INK ON PAPER
HANGING SCROLL, FRAMED, 46 × 64 CM
(LANDSCAPE), 29 × 64 CM (CALLIGRAPHY)
EA 1995.186

Title: 秋崖觀瀑 程十髮題
Watching the waterfall in the autumn mountains
Written by Cheng Shifa

Inscribed: 一九六三年八月抱石南京揮汗記
Painted by Fu Baoshi in the heat at Nanjing,
August 1963

Between 1961 and 1963 Fu Baoshi painted
numerous "watching the waterfall" scenes. This
example is typical in its use of a dry brush to depict
rushing water and in the mixture of pigment with
ink to produce brownish tones; its relatively small
scale and the addition of a title are however
unusual.

20   FU BAOSHI 傅抱石
1904–65

Landscape

INK AND SLIGHT COLOUR ON PAPER
HANGING SCROLL, 49 × 89 CM
EA 1995.187

Inscribed   甲申正月東川金剛坡下 抱石
1944, Dongchuan Jin'gangpo, Baoshi.

The developed foreground of windswept bamboo,
the relatively large proportions of the principal
figure and the weather itself combine to lend this
work an immediacy which is at variance with the
static qualities of more traditional landscape
painting. The inscription is in the style of characters
cast on ancient bronze vessels and the place
mentioned in it, Jin'gangpo, is in the vicinity of
Chongqing where Fu lived between 1937 and
1945.

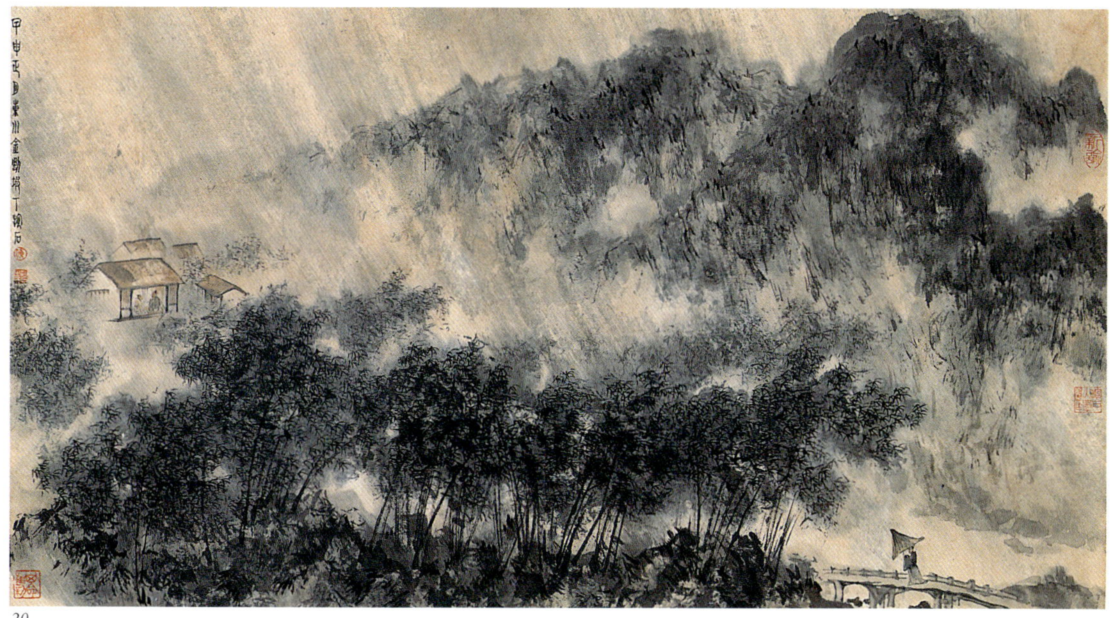

20

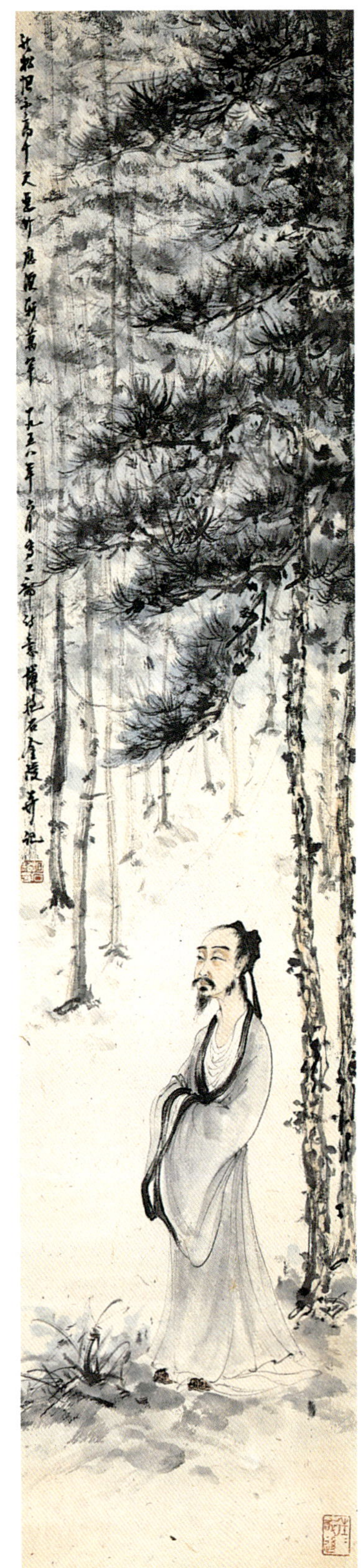

21

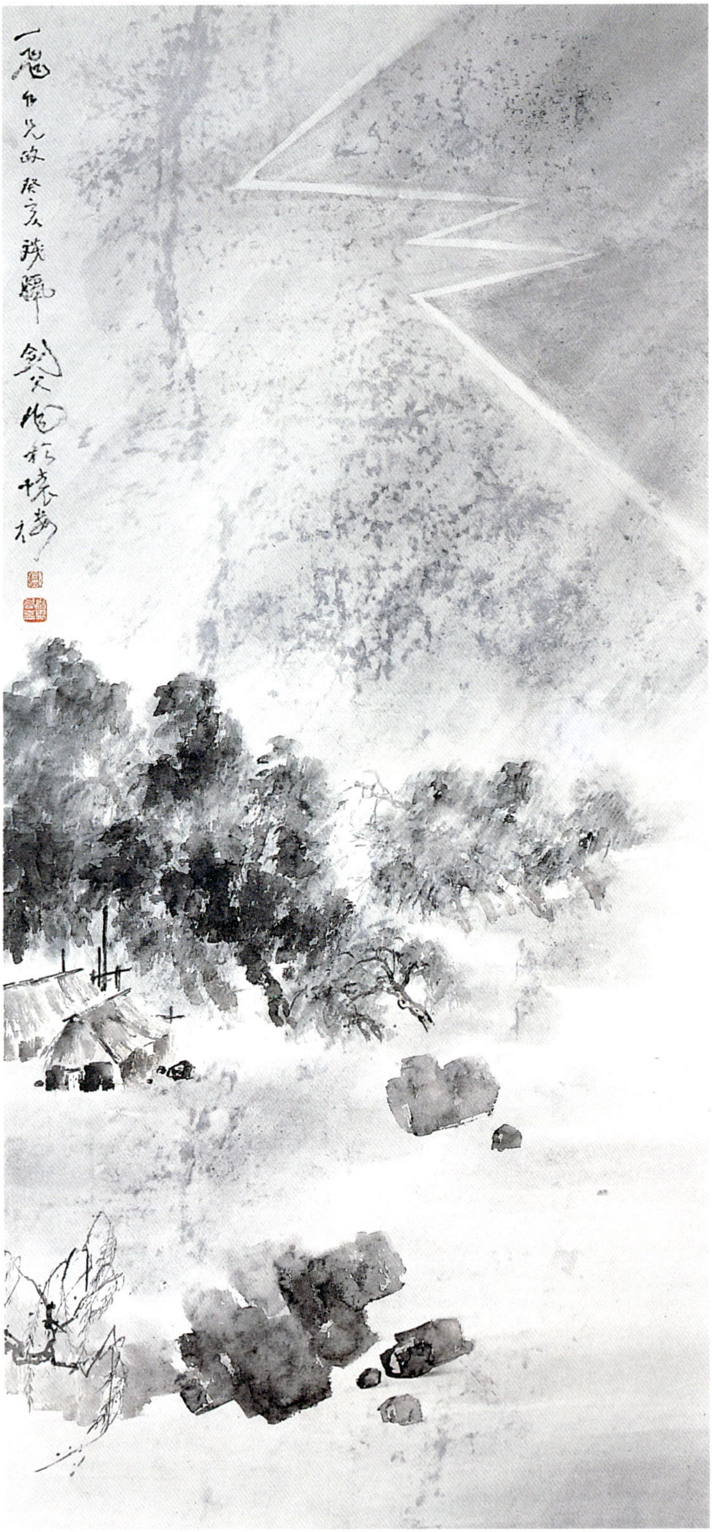

22

21 FU BAOSHI 傅抱石
1904–65

The poet Du Fu

INK AND COLOUR ON PAPER
HANGING SCROLL, 104 × 23 CM
EA 1995.188

Inscribed: 新松恨不高千尺　惡竹應須斬萬竿
一九五八年　六月寫工部詩意　傅抱石金陵幷記

(couplet transcribed from a poem by Du Fu)
Describing the poem, June 1958, Fu Baoshi at Nanjing

The famous Tang dynasty poet Du Fu (712–70) from Sichuan province was the subject of many figure paintings by Fu Baoshi. The first was painted for the poet's former residence in Chengdu while a version in Nanjing Museum and another, in a private collection, are both dated 1964 and bear the same inscription as the present painting.

22 GAO JIANFU 高劍父
1879–1951

Landscape

INK AND SLIGHT COLOUR ON PAPER
HANGING SCROLL, 130.2 × 62.5 CM
EA 1995.189

Inscribed: 一飛仁兄改癸亥殘臘　劍父作松懷樓
Painted for esteemed Yifei, the last days of the 12th month, 1923, by Jianfu at Songhuailou

Gao Jianfu is one of the Three Masters of the Lingnan School. He was concerned with the modernization of Chinese painting, both in terms of subject matter and of incorporating foreign styles; the bold lightning in this work owes more to Japanese design than traditional Chinese composition. *Songhuailou* in the inscription refers to the pavilion where the scroll was painted.

23 GAO MADE 高馬得
1918–

Scene from "White Snake"

INK AND COLOUR ON PAPER
ALBUM LEAF IN WESTERN MOUNT, FRAMED,
32.5 × 42.6 CM
EA 1995.190

Inscribed: 許郎何必尋煩惱　庚午夏月馬得畫　白蛇傳
驚變一折
Why should Master Xu bring vexation on himself? Painted (by) Made, summer 1990 White Snake's sudden transformation scene

Gao Made is a largely self-taught painter, influenced by Ye Qianyu and known as a cartoonist and illustrator of scenes from opera. The Peking opera "White Snake" tells of a heavenly snake turned beauty who marries a Master Xu. A knowing monk persuades Xu to give her drugged wine which will reveal her identity, and she is depicted here having just drunk it.

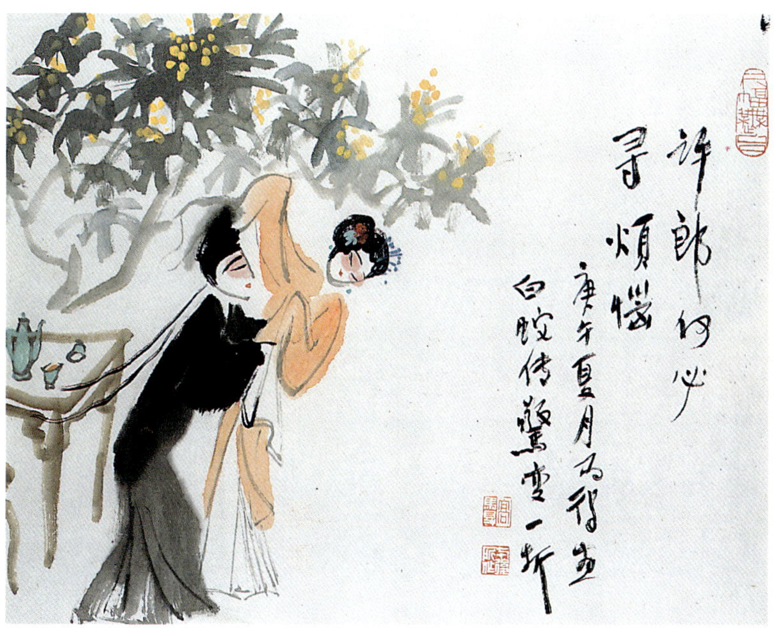

23

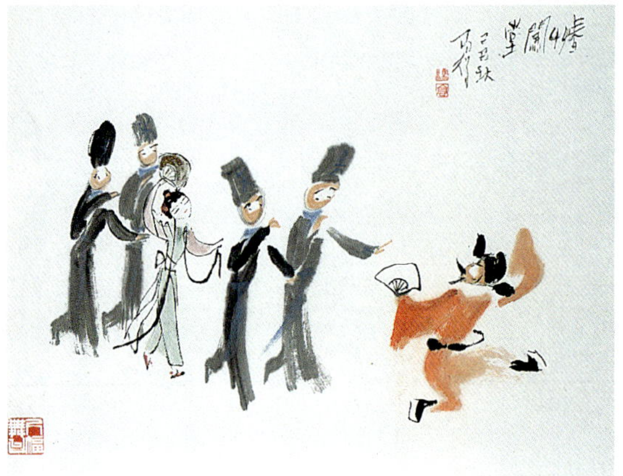

25 GAO MADE 高馬得
1918–

Chun Cao Outwits the Magistrate
春草闖堂

INK AND COLOUR ON PAPER
ALBUM LEAF IN WESTERN MOUNT, FRAMED,
33.5 × 43 CM

EA 1995.192

Inscribed: 己巳秋馬得   *autumn 1989,
Made*

Chun Cao Outwits the Magistrate is the title of a famous Peking opera in which the maid Chun Cao, on learning that a good man is to be sentenced to death, saves him by persuading the magistrate that he is betrothed to her mistress, the prime minister's daughter. The two eventually marry.

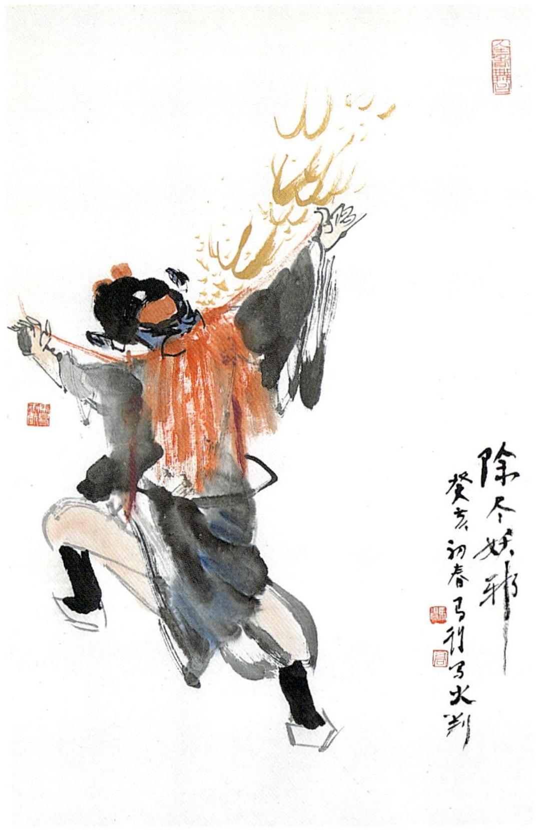

24 GAO MADE 高馬得
1918–

Quelling the Demons 除盡妖邪

INK AND COLOUR ON PAPER
HANGING SCROLL, FRAMED, 67.2 × 44 CM

EA 1995.191

Inscribed: 癸亥初春馬得寫火判
Early spring 1983 Made (painted) Huo Pan (Zhong Kui)

Zhong Kui the Demon Queller derives from Tang legend, having been a poor but ugly scholar in the reign of Emperor Minghuang (712–56), whose unprepossessing looks denied him the recognition his intellect deserved. He is a popular subject not just for professional illustrators such as Gao Made and Cheng Shifa (see cat.no.13), but also for other artists when producing figure paintings (see cat. no. 101). This particularly fiery Zhong Kui is depicted in the style of an opera figure.

26 GUAN LIANG 關良
1900–

Opera figure

INK AND COLOURS ON PAPER
HANGING SCROLL, FRAMED, 67.2 × 49.6 CM
EA 1995.193
Inscribed: 己未春　關良 , *Spring 1979, Guan Liang*

Guan Liang from Guangdong province is a
traditionally-trained painter specialising in opera
figures. His style is characterised by the use of
calligraphic ink line in conjunction with bold
colour. This painting depicts a combat scene, which
in Peking opera were always based on martial arts.

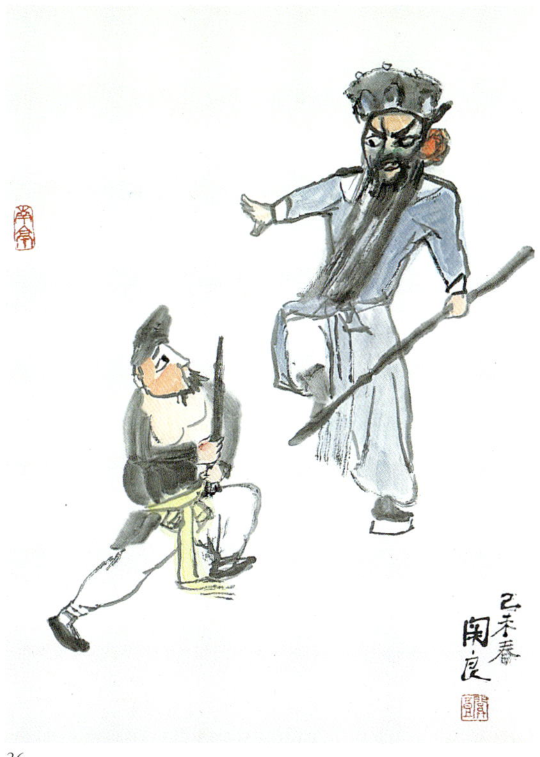

26

27 GUAN SHANYUE 關山月
1912–

Tree

INK AND COLOUR ON PAPER
HANGING SCROLL, FRAMED, 100.2 × 54.6 CM
EA 1995.194
Signed 　關山月畫 , *Painted (by) Guan Shanyue*

Guan Shanyue is an artist of the Lingnan School
from Canton who achieved national prominence and
painted landscapes from all over China. The tree, a
mangrove, is painted in traditional style with dense
ink, while the bright blue *dian* (dots) are typical of
the artist's use of that colour in the late 1980s.

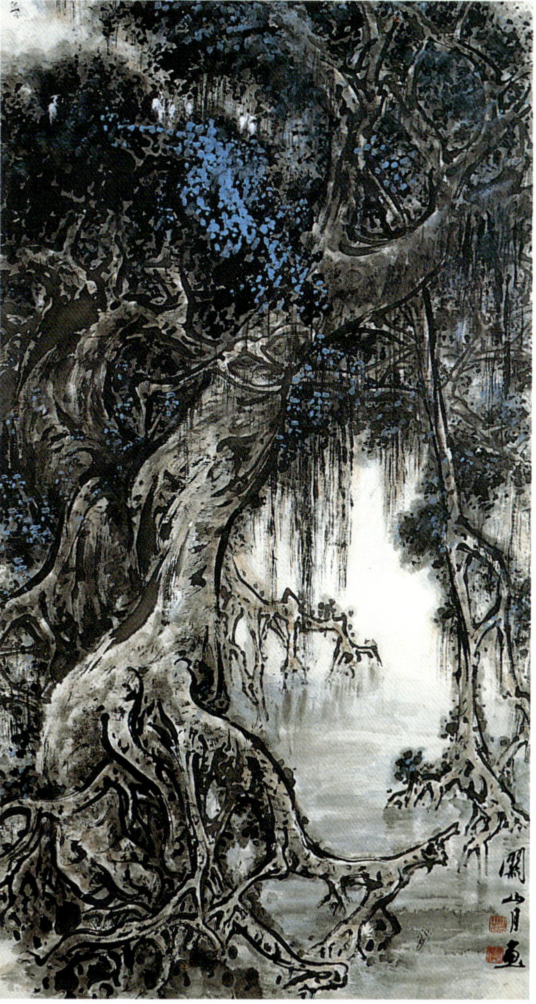

27

28 HUANG BAOYUE 黃保鉞
and TANG YUN 唐雲
1910–93

Calligraphy and bird

INK AND INK AND COLOUR ON PAPER
TWO ALBUM LEAVES MOUNTED TOGETHER,
FRAMED, 32 × 37.5 CM EACH

EA 1995.293 a,b

Inscribed: 節臨 ＿ 榮碑 青山老農葆鉞
*transcription of a portion of the inscription of Wu Rong
stele (by) Qingshan laonong Baoyue*

Inscribed: 丙戎夏六月杭人唐雲寫
*1946 summer, sixth month, written (by) Tang Yun
from Hangzhou*

The calligraphy is in lishu (clerical script) form and
is a transcription of part of the famous Wu Rong
stele at Ji'nan in Shandong province, carved in the
Han (206 BC–221 AD) dynasty. The bird is painted
in traditional decorative style, and was probably
mounted together with the calligraphy not long
after it was completed.

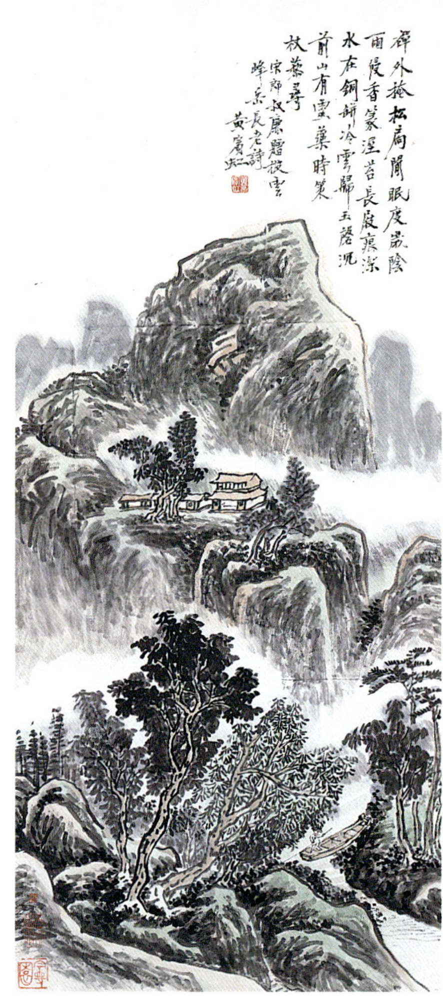

29

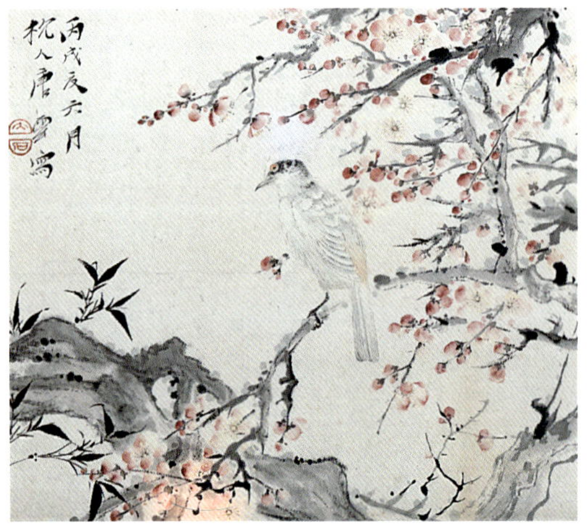

28

29 Attributed to
HUANG BINHONG 黃賓虹
1864–1955

Landscape

INK AND COLOUR ON PAPER
HANGING SCROLL, FRAMED, 79 × 34.2 CM

EA 1995.195

Inscribed: 40-character poem, followed by
宋郎叔廉贈披雲　岳長老詩 黃賓虹
*Transcription of a poem by a Song literatus, for
presentation to a monk Huang Binhong*

Huang Binhong was a prominent connoisseur, art
historian and administrator, and compiler of the
Meishu congshu (Encyclopaedia of Art). He was also
one of the leading traditional landscape painters of
the early twentieth century, and the present
example is in his typical style.

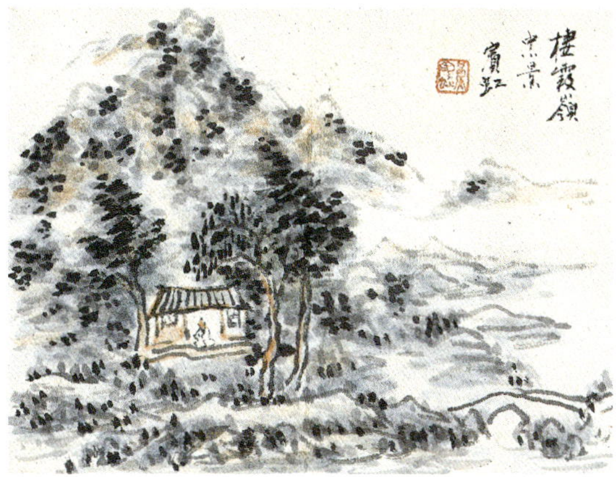

30

30   HUANG BINHONG 黃賓虹
1864–1955

Landscape

INK AND COLOUR ON PAPER
ALBUM OF EIGHT DOUBLE LEAVES, 13 × 9 CM
EA 1995.196
This leaf inscribed: 棲霞嶺中小景　賓虹
Scene in Xixia peak　　Binhong

This album includes views of mountain scenery in
different regions of China. The format is small, yet
Huang Binhong's landscape style of rich ink and
layered brushwork over a simple structure is evident.
It is for his development of traditional brushwork
that Huang Binhong has been particularly admired.

31   HUANG QIUYUAN 黃秋園
1914–79

Landscape

INK COLOUR ON PAPER
HANGING SCROLL, FRAMED, 133 × 68.4 CM
EA 1995.197
Inscribed: 28-character inscription followed by
甲寅初 ＿ 熱揮汗畫此以助涼氣　半個和尙老
＿ 年六十半個僧畫

*Early summer 1974 depicting this painting to cool
down Painted (by) the half-monk, age 60*

Huang Qiuyuan from Jiangxi devoted himself to
painting only after retiring from a banking career,
and it was not until some years after his death that
his work achieved recognition. The tight composition of this work, its lengthy inscription and fibrous
yellow paper are all typical features of his paintings.

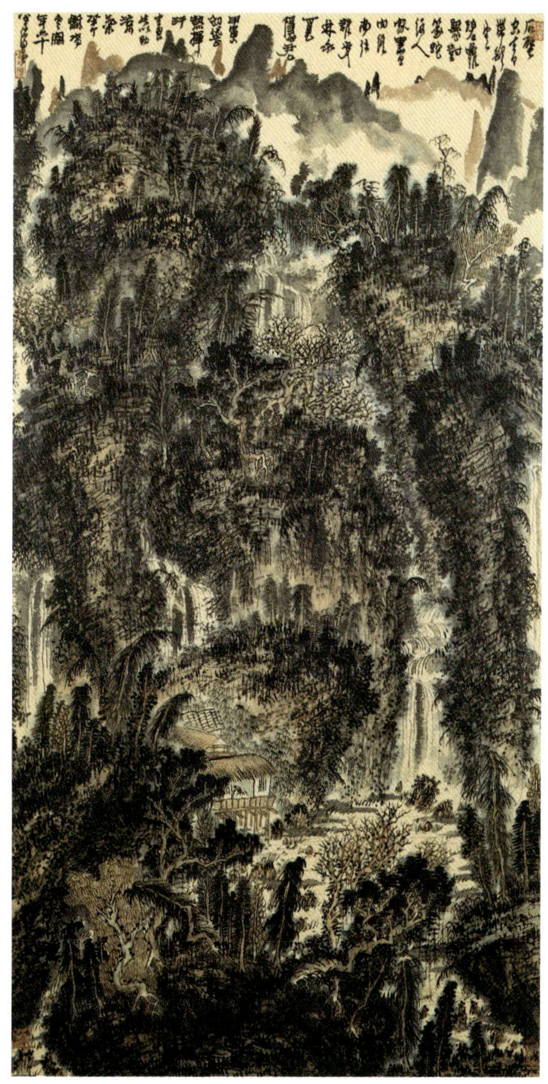

31

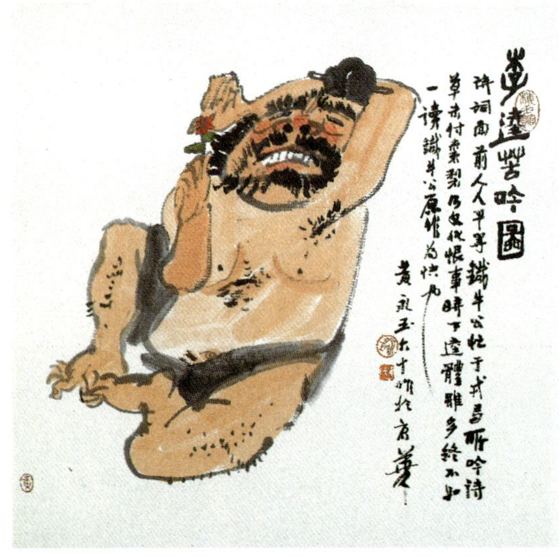

32

33 HUANG YONGYU 黃永玉
1924–

Lotus

INK AND COLOUR ON PAPER
HANGING SCROLL, FRAMED, 127 × 66.4 CM
EA 1995.199
Signed 永玉 Yongyu

Huang Yongyu from Hunan now lives in Hong Kong and worked originally as a woodcut artist. His paintings are frequently bold in both statement and colour, and often include experimental media. He has produced many colourful lotus flowers like these, in a variety of palettes.

32 HUANG YONGYU 黃永玉
1924–

Li Kui reciting poetry with difficulty
李逵苦吟圖

INK AND COLOUR ON PAPER
HANGING SCROLL, FRAMED, 67.2 × 67.2 CM
EA 1995.198

Inscribed: 56-character inscription ending
黃永玉六十作于京華
Done by Huang Yongyu, sixty, in the capital

Li Kui is a rough and ready outlaw in the 14th-century popular novel *Shuihu zhuan* (The Water Margin), a fighter rather than a poet. Huang Yongyu laments in the inscription that Li Kui's poems were never written down, while those of his modern equivalents abound. Huang Yongyu painted at least two more versions of this subject in the same year, 1984, while in Beijing.

34 HUANG YONGYU 黃永玉
1924–

Wu Lu challenged by Zhu Yun
五鹿嶽嶽朱雲折其角

INK AND COLOUR ON PAPER
HANDSCROLL, 67 × 138 CM
EA 1995.296

Inscribed: 黃永玉作于鳳凰
Done (by) Huang Yongyu at Fenghuang

The subject of this painting is two Han (206 BC–AD 220) dynasty debaters, the supremo Wu Lu (literally Five Deer) and the younger Zhu Yun (Vermilion Cloud), described in the title as "breaking his horn". It is not clear who will succeed in this discussion, only that eventually Zhu Yun will be the greater debater. The force of the debate is evident in the dynamic sweeping brushstrokes, while the faces and hands perhaps represent the finer points of the argument. Fenghuang is Huang Yongyu's native district in Hunan province.

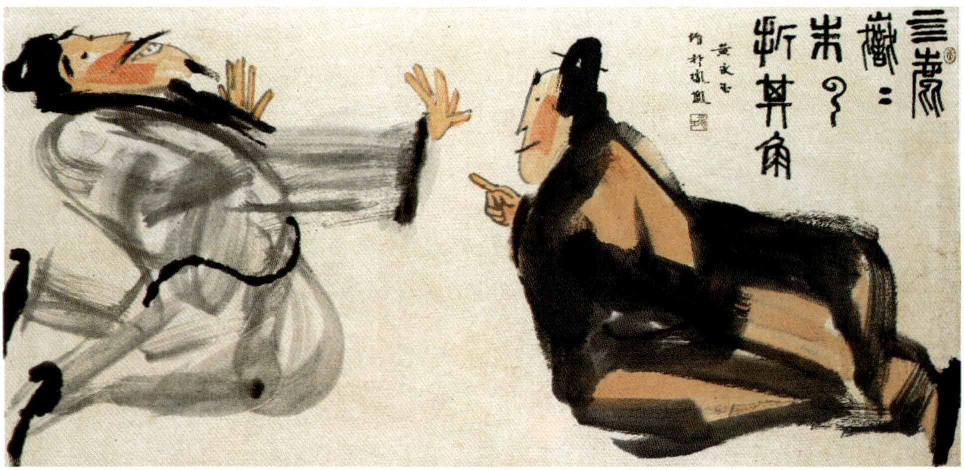

34

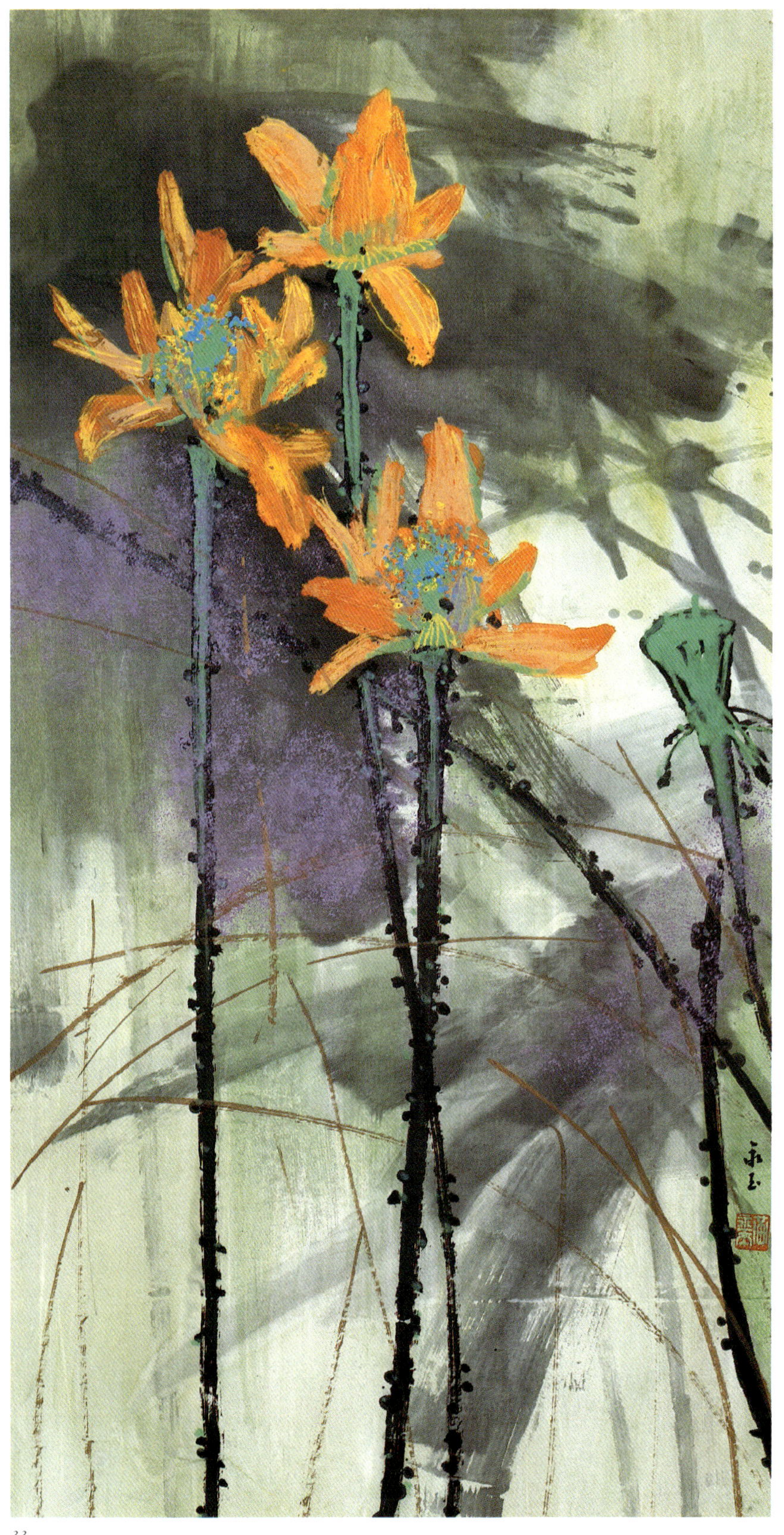

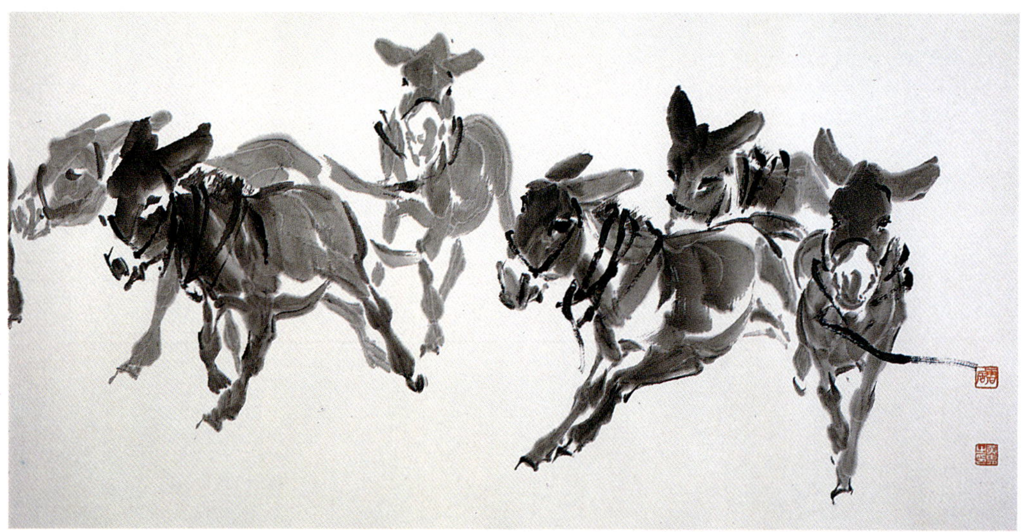

35 HUANG ZHOU 黃冑
1925–

Nineteen donkeys

INK ON PAPER
HANDSCROLL, 43 × 273 CM
EA 1995.200
Inscribed, signed, and dated 1986

Huang Zhou is a self-taught painter of ethnic minority figures and animals. He is particularly well-known for his ink monochrome donkey paintings, which in the late 1970s were presented to foreign heads of state, and often depict such a profusion that the animals become difficult to count.

36 JACKSON YU 尤紹曾
1911–

Nude

INK AND COLOUR ON PAPER
VERTICAL PAINTING IN WESTERN MOUNT,
FRAMED, 33 × 28 CM
1995.201
Signed: 子玄 *Yu Xuan*

Jackson Yu was a leading member of the Circle Art Group in Hong Kong in the 1960s. For the following two decades he painted only in traditional style, and for recreation, but since the late 1980s he has produced paintings in western style. Many are in bright acrylics while some, as here, are executed in the traditional Chinese palette of ink and light colour.

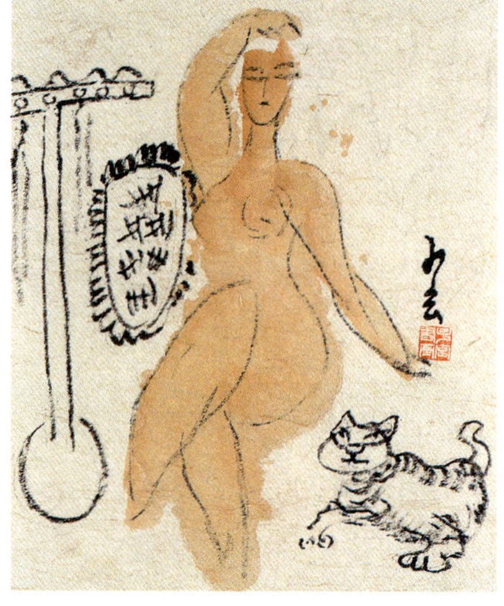

36

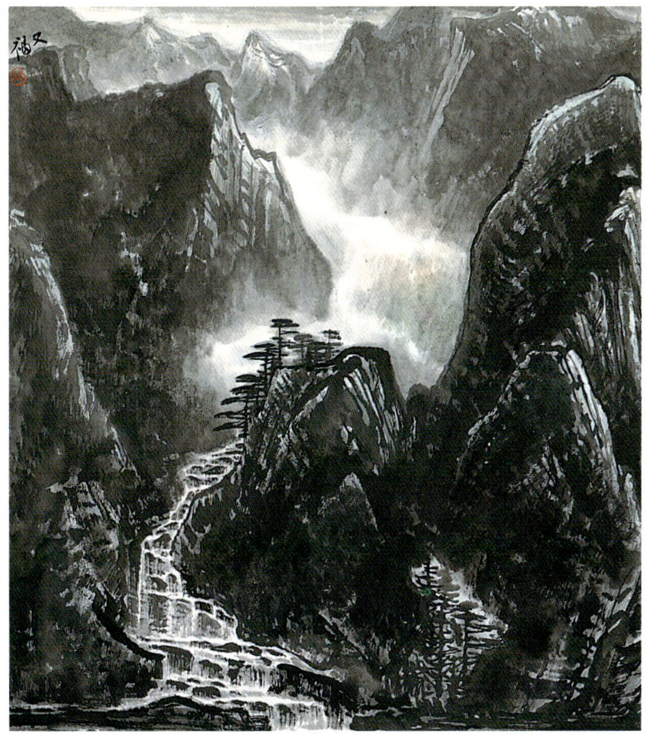

37

37　JIA YOUFU　賈又福
1942–

Mountain landscape

INK AND SLIGHT COLOUR ON PAPER
HANGING SCROLL, FRAMED, 64.4 × 57.5 CM
EA 1995.202
Signed: 又福　*Youfu*

Jia Youfu was a pupil of Li Keran (1907–89) and this painting, with its dense composition and heavy use of dark ink, may be regarded as a homage to his teacher (see cat.nos.43,46). The scene is probably a waterfall in the Taihang mountain range in north China, which since 1977 has been one of Jia Youfu's principal painting subjects.

38　KAN TAI-KEUNG　靳埭強
1942–

Landscape

INK AND COLOUR ON PAPER
HORIZONTAL SCROLL, FRAMED, 73.2 × 97.7 CM
EA 1995.203
Signed: 埭強九一年　*Daiqiang 1991*

Though born in Guangdong province, Kan moved to Hong Kong at the age of fifteen and his use of brightly coloured washes to depict traditional landscape forms is typical of the synthetic style of eastern and western painting that has emerged there.

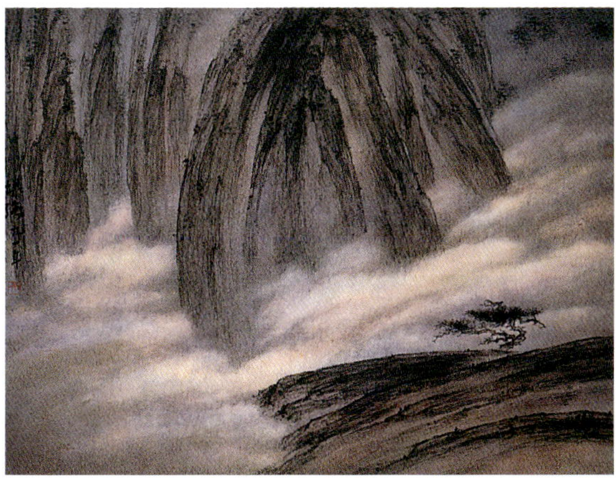

38

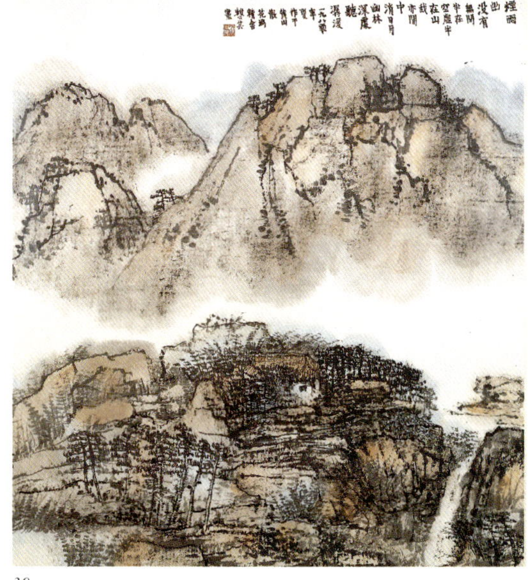

39

39 LAI SHAOQI 賴少其
1915–

Landscape

INK AND COLOUR ON PAPER

HANGING SCROLL, FRAMED, 96 × 89 CM

EA 1995.204

Inscribed: 47-character inscription ending
一九八零年夏作于黃山散花塢精舍　賴少其畫

*Painted by Lai Shaoqi while at Sanhuawu, Mt.
Huang, summer 1980*

Lai Shaoqi from Guangdong province was
originally a print artist. His landscape paintings
often depict Huangshan (Mount Huang) in Anhui
province and the composition of this work, broken
by cloud in the middle ground, is typical. The
square style of calligraphy is inspired by the 18th-
century Yangzhou painters Zheng Xie and,
particularly, Jin Nong.

40 LI HUASHENG 李華生
1941–

Crossing the River Ning at Night
寧河晚渡

INK AND COLOUR ON PAPER

HORIZONTAL SCROLL, FRAMED, 40.1 × 58.8 CM

EA 1995.205

Inscribed: 甲寅之秋余曾架鐵舟夜渡寧河
江上秋風空中皓月至今未忘也　鐵舟又名神駁兒
因其堅實如鐵故以鐵舟呼之　己未年春華生時
客北京

*59-character inscription ending Spring 1979,
Huasheng while staying in Beijing*

Li Huasheng from Sichuan was a pupil of Chen
Zizhuang (1913–76), and has a reputation as a
modern eccentric in the mode of the wilder Ming
and Qing artists. He often tends towards abstraction
while still producing quieter, more naturalistic paintings in a rustic vein, such as this moonlit landscape.

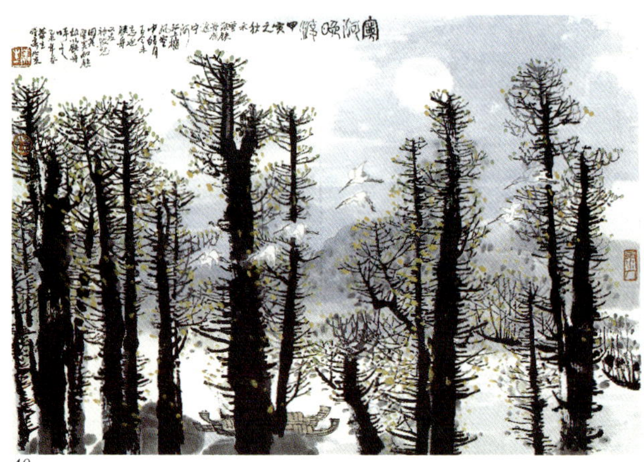

40

41   LI HUASHENG 李華生
1941–

Autumn River 秋江

INK AND COLOUR ON PAPER
HANGING SCROLL, FRAMED, 133 × 65.5 CM
EA 1995.206

Inscribed: 秋江歲在甲子時立冬巴人華生寫
Painted in winter 1984 (by) Li Huasheng of Sichuan

Li Huasheng's training in decorative painting is
evident in the composition of this work while his
unusual preference for yellow in landscapes appears
here in the form of the dotting that accentuates the
trees. The use of bright *dian* in other colours
appears in another landscape, below, and in the
works of Bao Chenchu, Guan Shanyue and Xie
Zhiliu (see cat.nos.1,27,97).

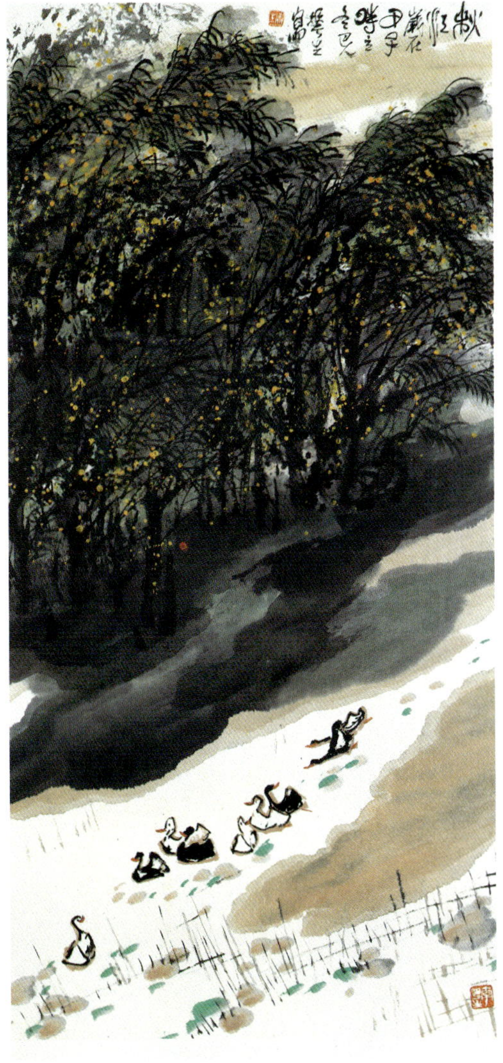

41

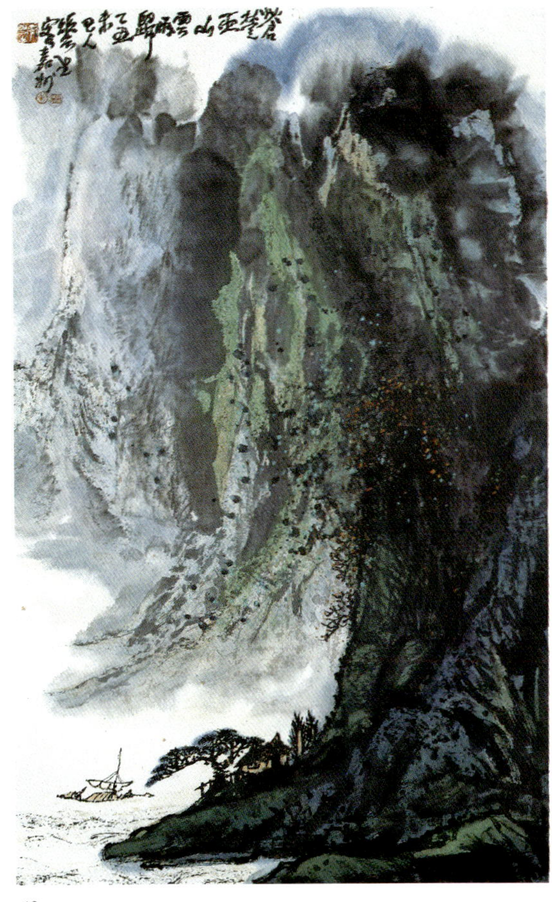

42

42   LI HUASHENG 李華生
1941–

Landscape

INK AND COLOUR ON PAPER
HANGING SCROLL, FRAMED

EA 1995.207

Inscribed: 蒼楚巫山雲雨歸 乙丑末巴人華生客嘉州
*Returning from Wushan in ancient Chu in mist and
rain, late 1985, Li Huasheng of Sichuan while
staying at Jiazhou*

Wushan (Mount Wu) is amongst the Yangzi gorges
in eastern Sichuan province. The huge cliff, the
darkened green and blue traditional landscape
colours and the swirling water convey the danger of
the river at this point. Li Huasheng's father was a
Yangzi boatman and Li himself was deeply
impressed by the river, making it the subject of
several large paintings during the late 1970s and
1980s.

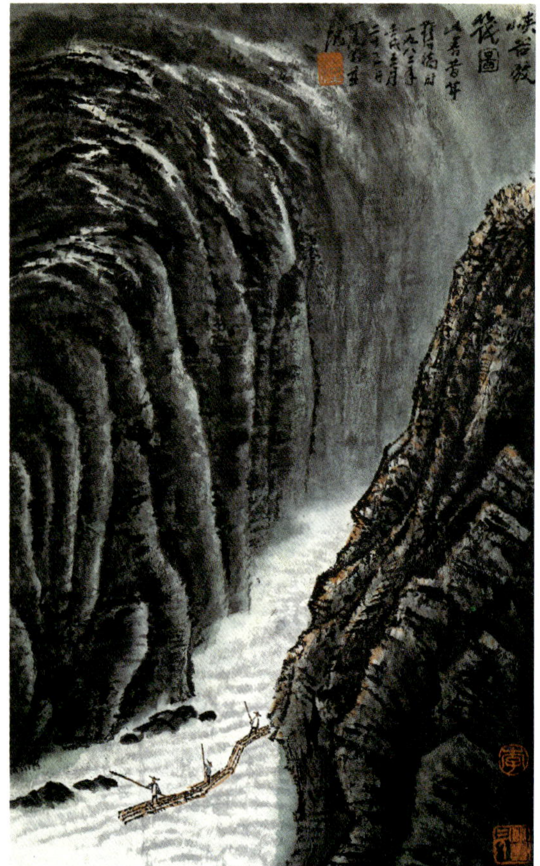

43

44   LI KERAN 李可染
1907–89

Whiling Away Summer at the Lotus Pond 荷塘消暑圖

INK AND SLIGHT COLOUR ON PAPER

HANGING SCROLL, 69 × 47 CM

EA 1995.209

Inscribed: 碧樹沉沉覆草堂, 湘簾齊揭藕風涼
六月無地避炎暑 安得移家住上方 一九八五年歲次
乙丑夏六月上浣 可染于師牛堂

*48-character inscription ending Early June 1985
Keran at the Shiniu Tang*

Li Keran first painted this subject in the late 1940s;
he is known for producing repetitive works (see
cat.no.43, inscription) and three further versions of
this painting, with closely similar composition and
inscriptions, share the same title and date as this
scroll. Li Keran was an advocate of painting
outdoors but towards the end of his life ill health
forced him to work in his studio, the Shiniu Tang.

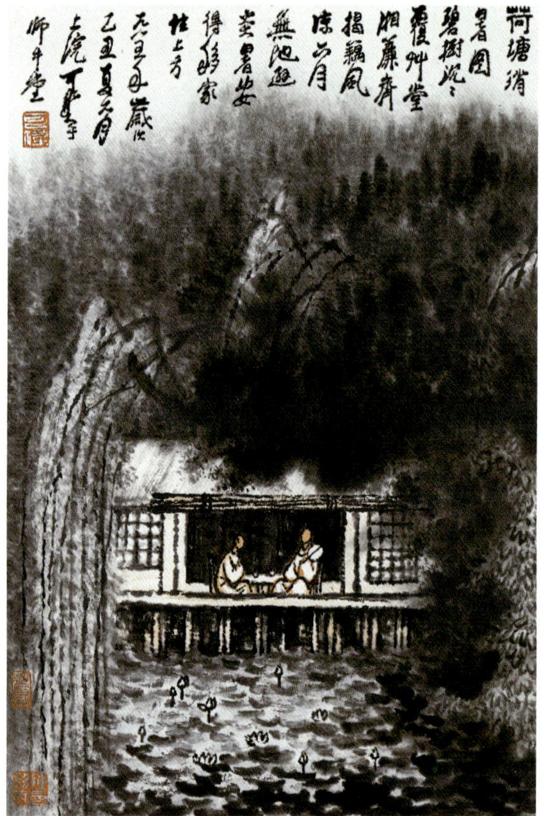

44

43   LI KERAN 李可染
1907–89

Rafts in a Gorge 峽谷放筏圖

INK AND SLIGHT COLOUR ON PAPER

HANGING SCROLL, FRAMED, 66.7 × 42.2 CM

EA 1995.208

Inscribed: 此吾昔年舊稿時一九八二年壬戌六月
二十五日 可染幷記

*This I have sketched in previous years 25 June 1982
Keran*

Li Keran is one of the leading traditional painters of
the 20th century, and studied with Huang
Binhong, Qi Baishi and Lin Fengmian. The fullness
of the composition and the repeating forms of the
mountains are typical of his landscape style, while
the large areas of dark ink are a feature of his later
works.

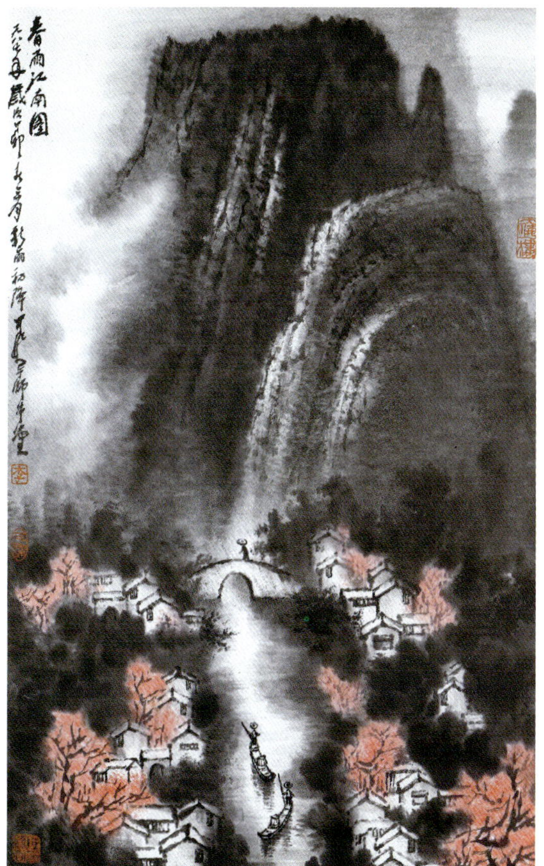

45

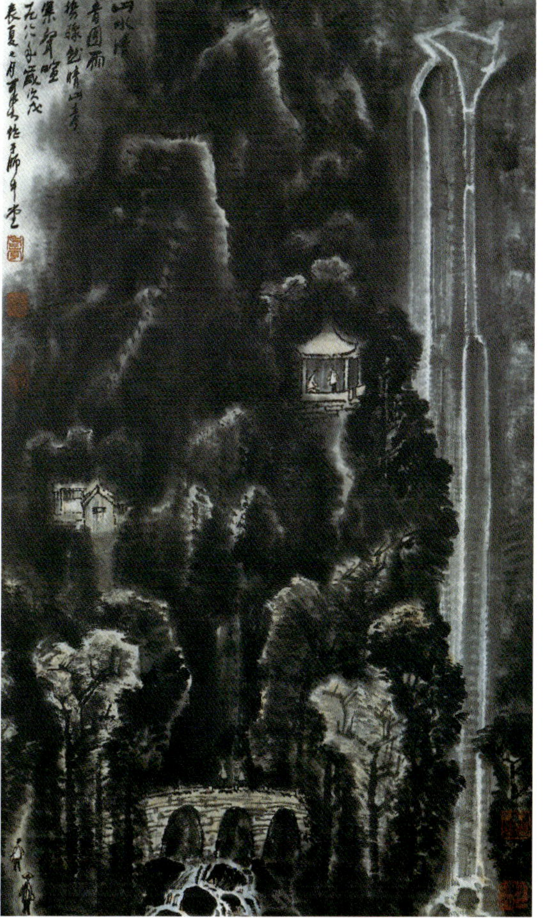

46

45　LI KERAN　李可染
1907–89

Spring Rain in Jiangnan 春雨江南圖

INK AND COLOUR ON PAPER
HANGING SCROLL, 89 × 58 CM
EA 1995.210

Inscribed:　一九八七年歲次丁卯春三月新雨初
降　可染于師牛堂

*1987, spring, the third month, the first rainfall, Keran
at the Shiniu Tang*

Li Keran painted landscapes in this style, with tall
mountains in wet ink enlivened with white houses
and pink blossom in the foreground, from at least
the early 1970s; another version of the present
painting is dated 1988.

46　LI KERAN　李可染
1907–89

Clear Sounds in the Landscape
山水清音圖

INK AND SLIGHT COLOUR ON PAPER
HANGING SCROLL, FRAMED, 92.6 × 54.1 CM
EA 1995.211

Inscribed:　雨勢驟然晴山青　聲喧
一九八八年歲次戊辰夏七月　可染作于師牛堂

*a couplet, followed by 1988, summer, seventh
month, done (by) Keran at the Shiniu Tang*

The dark wet ink and full, almost decoratively
balanced composition are typical of Li Keran's landscapes. In addition to landscapes, Li is particularly
known for paintings of herdboys and buffalo, after
which his studio *Shiniu Tang* "Hall of learning from
the buffalo" takes its name.

47 LI KERAN 李可染
1907–89

Calligraphy couplet

INK ON PAPER

PAIR OF HANGING SCROLLS, 136 × 34 CM EACH

EA 1995.295 a,b

Inscribed: 蕭軍同志正　一九八五歲次乙丑六月白發
—— 李可染　書于師牛堂

*For Mr. Xiao Jun　June 1985 written (by) Li Keran
at Shiniu Tang*

Li Keran, whose own parents were illiterate, had no
formal training in calligraphy but taught himself by
copying from rubbings of Han (206 BC–AD 220)
dynasty writing and from characters written outside
shops. The couplet translates, "When I write the
word "palm leaf" the essay becomes green, when I
use the words "plum blossom" the whole couplet
becomes fragrant".

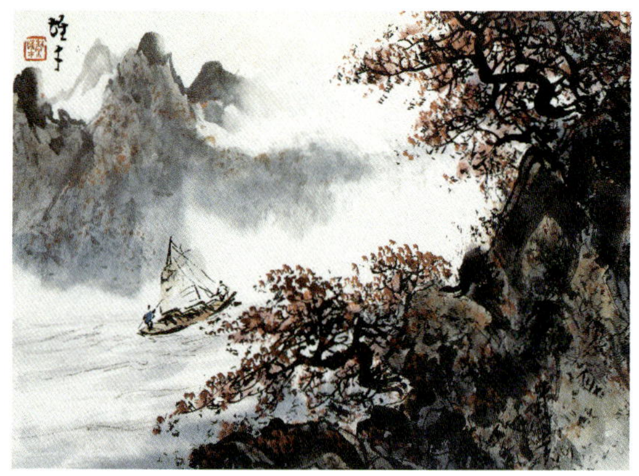

48

48 LI XIONGCAI 黎雄才
1910–

Landscape

INK AND COLOUR ON PAPER

HANGING SCROLL, FRAMED, 34.3 × 45 CM

EA 1995.212

Signed　雄才　*Xiongcai*

Li Xiongcai from Guangdong province was a pupil
of the Lingnan master Gao Jianfu (1879–1951). His
landscapes are traditional in style and the use of
dark ink with a dry brush, as in the foreground of
this painting, is a typical feature of his work.

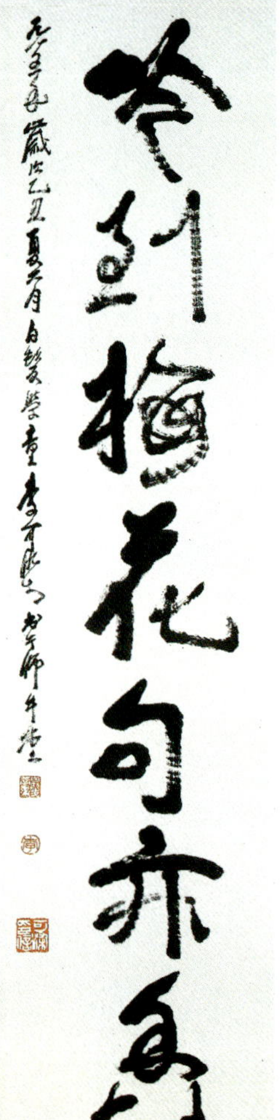

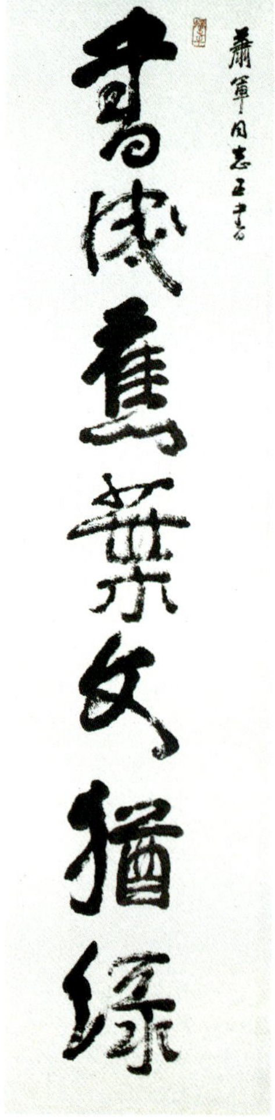

47

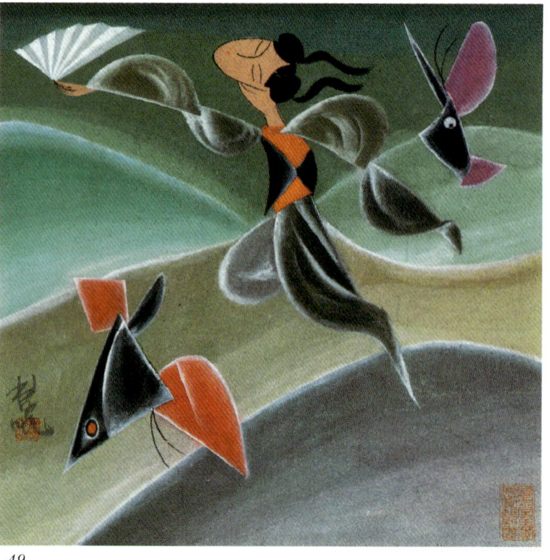

49

49 LIN FENGMIAN 林風眠
1900–91

Dancing figure

INK AND COLOUR ON PAPER
HANGING SCROLL, FRAMED, 34 × 34 CM
EA 1995.213
Signed: 林風眠   *Lin Fengmian*

Lin Fengmian from Guangdong province was one of the leading modern Chinese painters of the twentieth century, a reformer who led the Hangzhou National Art Academy in the 1930s. In this painting he appears to be experimenting with reduction of form and use of colour in ways hitherto unseen in China.

50 LIN FENGMIAN 林風眠
1900–91

Landscape

INK AND COLOUR ON PAPER
SQUARE PAINTING IN CHINESE MOUNT, FRAMED, 68 × 69.7 CM
EA 1995.214
Signed: 林風眠   *Lin Fengmian*

This colourful landscape with its square format retains an essentially Chinese composition. Lin's synthetic style is based in his view that Chinese art is strong on expression of ideas though not on form, while Western painting excelled in representation but lacked expressiveness.

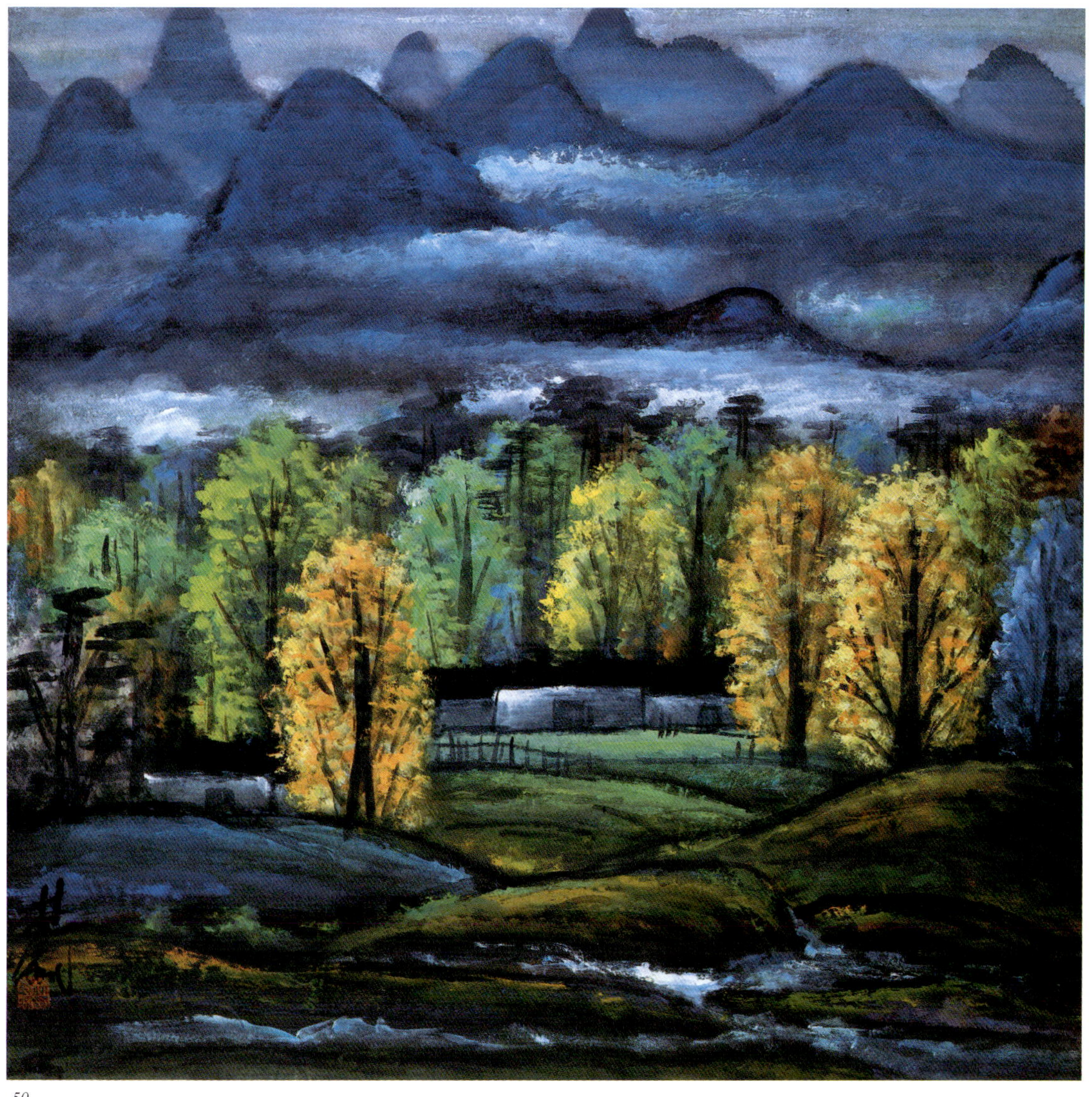

50

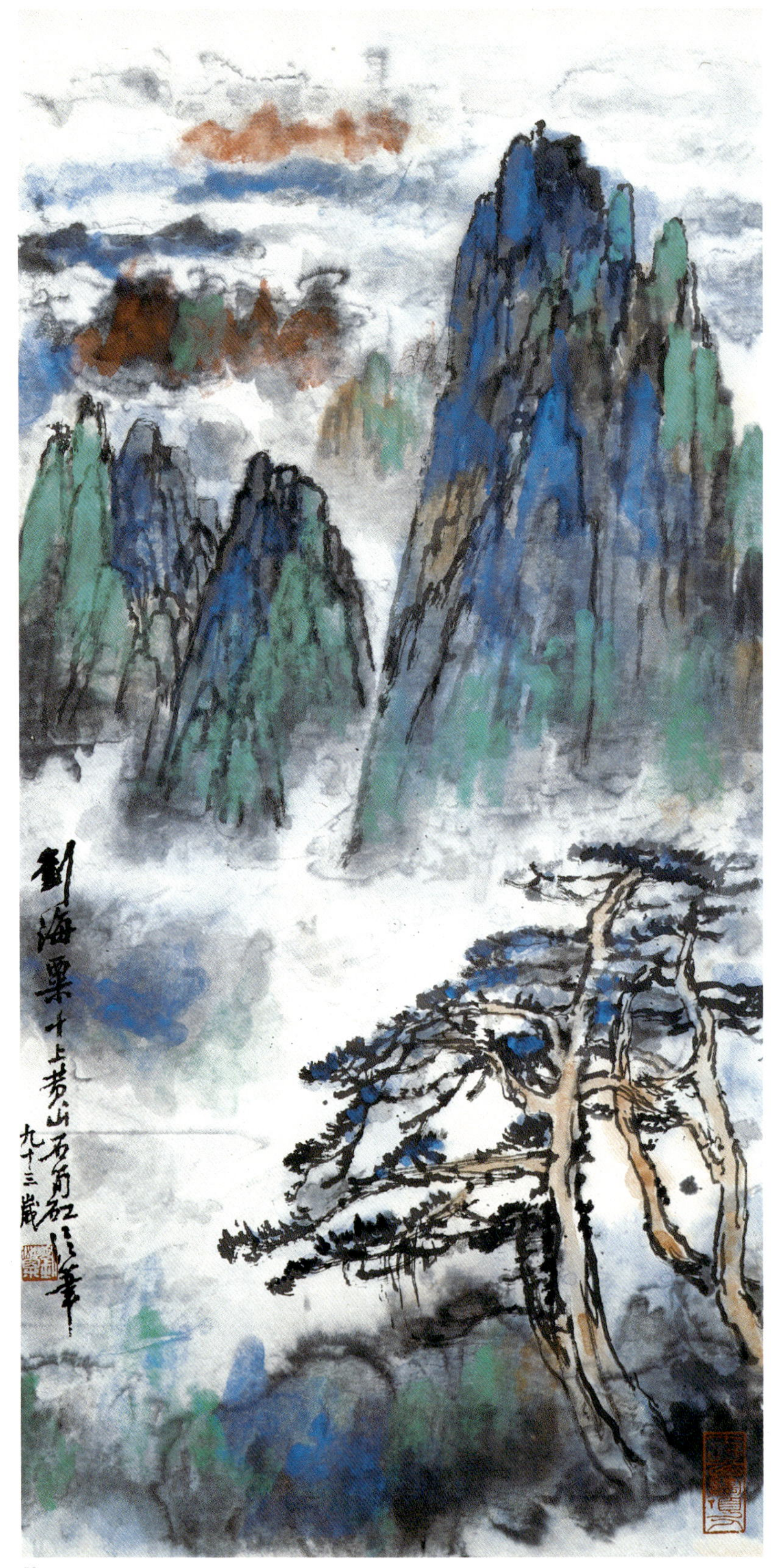

52

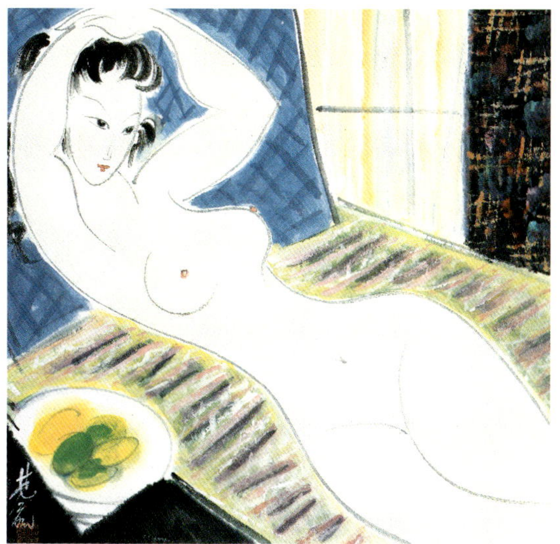

51

51   LIN FENGMIAN   林風眠
1900–91

Nude, after Matisse

INK AND COLOUR ON PAPER
PAINTING IN CHINESE MOUNT, FRAMED,
49.5 × 52 CM
EA 1995.215
Signed: 林風眠   *Lin Fengmian*

This nude in the style of Matisse reflects the ten years (1918-28) Lin Fengmian spent in Paris as a young artist deeply influenced by Fauvism and the Parisian avant-garde. Many Chinese artists subsequently learned Western techniques through producing imitative works of this type.

52   LIU HAISU   劉海粟
1896–1994

Landscape

INK AND COLOUR ON PAPER
HANGING SCROLL, FRAMED, 120 × 60.1 CM
EA 1995.216

Inscribed: 劉海粟十上黃山石筍 __ 信筆 九十三歲
Drawn by Liu Haisu at Shisun _, Mt. Huang, age ninety-three".

Liu Haisu was one of the leading reformers of traditional painting. He founded the Shanghai Art Academy in 1912 when he was sixteen, and later trained in Europe. The juxtaposition of strong splashed colours in this painting derives from his experience with oils, and they are here combined with traditional ink to portray the famous sacred mountain, Huangshan, which was a favoured subject of Liu Haisu in his later years.

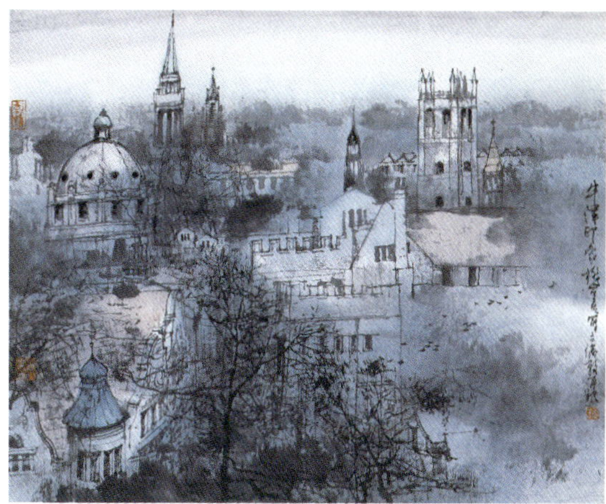

53

53   LIU MAOSHAN   劉懋善
1942–

Views of Oxford and Cambridge

INK AND COLOUR ON PAPER
PAIR OF ALBUM LEAVES, MOUNTED AS
HANGING SCROLL, EACH 47.5 × 59.4 CM
EA 1995.217 a,b
Inscribed:
a) 牛津印象   懋善寫於倫敦并記
Impression of Oxford   Painted in London (by) Maoshan
b) 懋善於劍橋寫生
Painted at the scene in Cambridge (by) Maoshan

Liu Maoshan from Jiangsu province studied European drawing before taking up traditional Chinese ink painting. Since 1990 he has travelled in the United States and Europe, producing many views of famous monuments and small towns in the style of these album leaves.

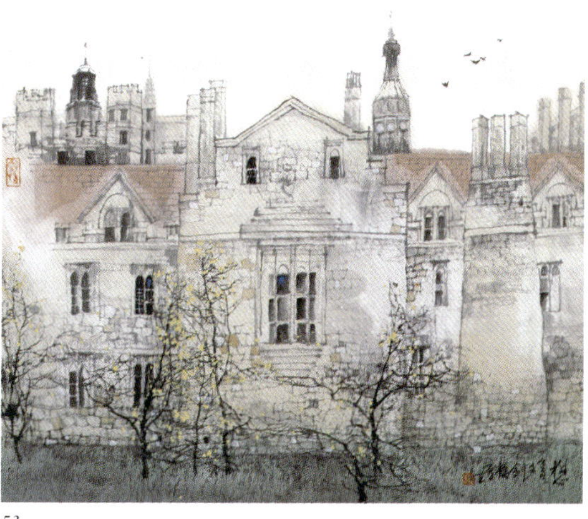

53

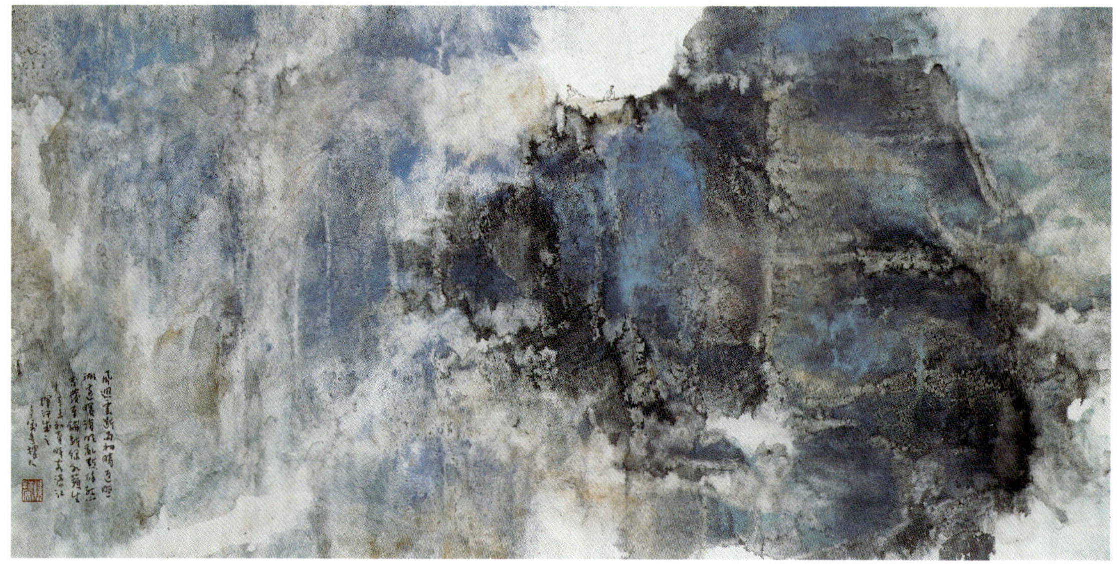

54

54 LOU BAI'AN
(LAO PAK ON) 樓柏安
1947–

Blue and Green Landscape

INK AND COLOUR ON PAPER

HORIZONTAL SCROLL IN WESTERN MOUNT,
FRAMED, 62.5 × 128.8 CM

EA 1995.218

Inscribed: 28-character poem, followed by
辛未初夏　時客濠江揮汗成之萬豐樓人
*Completed in early summer 1991 while staying at _
jiang, Wan Feng Lou Ren*

Lou Bai'an moved from Zhejiang province to
Macau in 1981 and is now resident in Taiwan. He
is renowned as a calligrapher, and in landscape
painting for his use of large areas of colour. The
forms of this landscape are almost unrepresentational;
only the two seated figures enable the viewer to
understand the painting as a Chinese landscape.

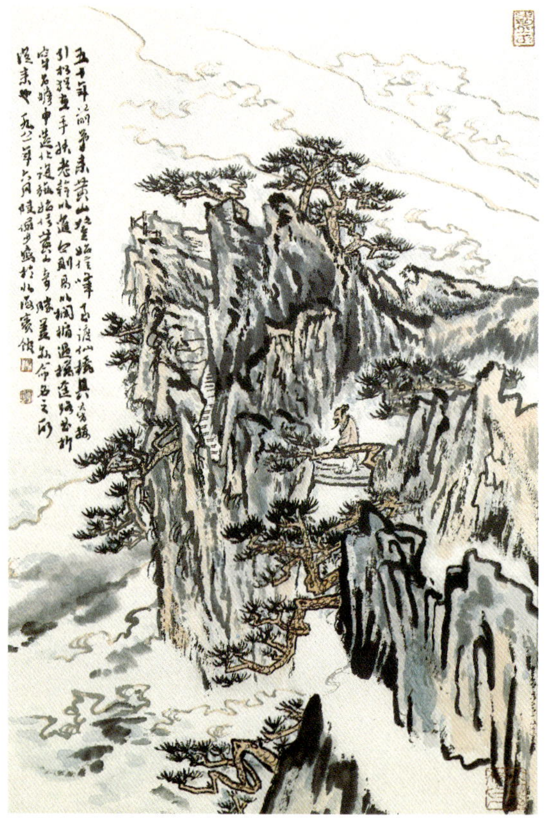

55

55   LU YANSHAO　陸儼少
1909–93

Landscape

INK AND COLOUR ON PAPER
VERTICAL PAINTING IN WESTERN MOUNT,
FRAMED, 66.2 × 44.5 CM
EA 1995.219
Inscribed:
80-character inscription ending
一九八一年六月陸儼少寫於北海賓館
1981, June, drawn (by) Lu Yanshao at Beihai guest house

The inscription discusses Mount Huang in Anhui province, the sacred mountain Lu Yanshao first visited as a young man and which is depicted in many of his landscapes. Lu Yanshao painted within the classical tradition and his own style is noted for the diagonal sense of movement evident in this work.

56   LU YANSHAO　陸儼少
1909–93

Landscape

INK ON PAPER
ALBUM LEAF, MOUNTED, 34 × 38.7 CM
EA 1995.220
Inscribed:
50-character inscription ending
一九七八年五月陸儼少
1978, May, Lu Yanshao

Lu Yanshao is credited with several innovative techniques in landscape painting, and the use of dark and pale wet ink together in the background of the present composition is an example. The restlessness that characterises his style is evident even in this simple album leaf.

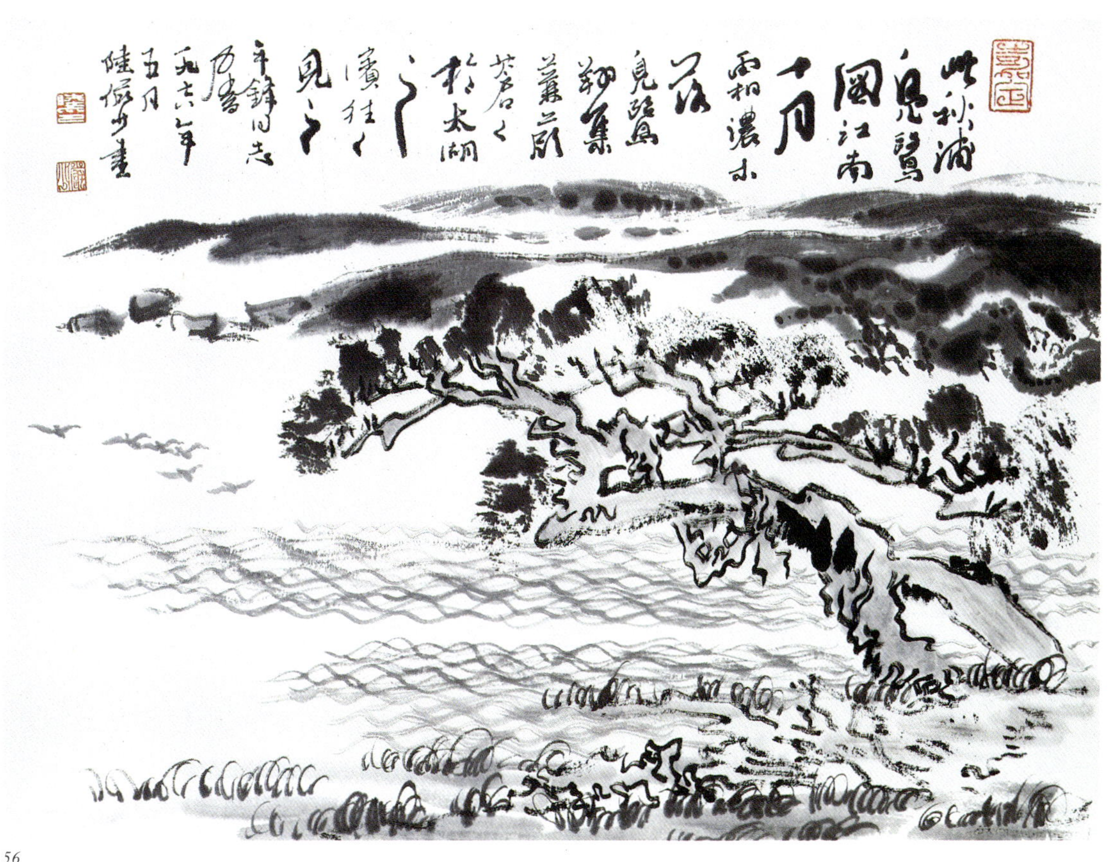

57   LU YANSHAO 陸儼少
1909–93

Plum blossom

INK AND COLOUR ON PAPER
HANGING SCROLL, FRAMED, 96.5 × 60.8 CM
EA 1995.221

Inscribed: 37-character inscription ending
一九七九年十二月陸儼少寫于西子湖濱
1979, December, drawn (by) Lu Yanshao on the bank of West Lake

This is a large version of a subject Lu Yanshao often chose for the smaller format of album leaf. The outlining of the blossoms in a very pale grey ink eliminates the decorative associations of flower painting, while the general style is consistent with that of his landscapes.

58   MISCELLANEOUS ARTISTS
of the late Qing and Republican periods

Landscapes, birds and flowers

INK AND INK AND COLOUR ON PAPER
TWELVE FAN PAINTINGS, EACH L. 50 CM
APPROX.
EA 1995.222 a–l

The seven landscapes and five bird-and-flower paintings are mostly typical of conservative, amateur painting from the mid-19th to early 20th century. The painting illustrated here is signed *Old man shihu* and dedicated to a Mr. Chun. The recipient may have been known to the artist personally, or may simply have commissioned a painting; fan paintings were often quickly painted to order, and as such seldom represent the artist's most serious work.

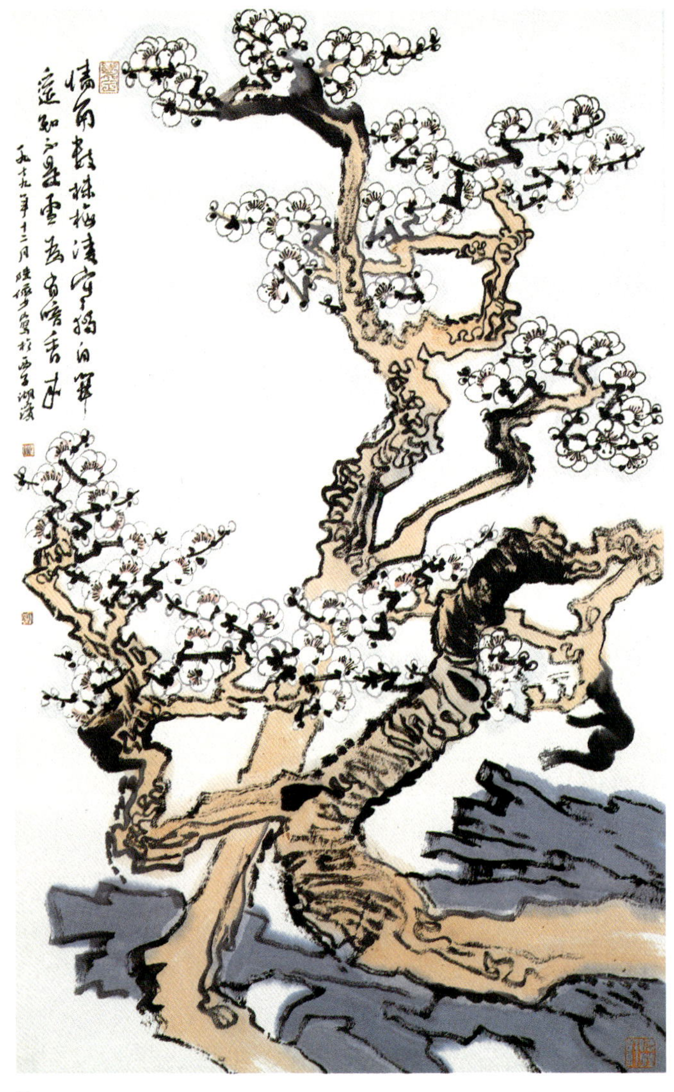

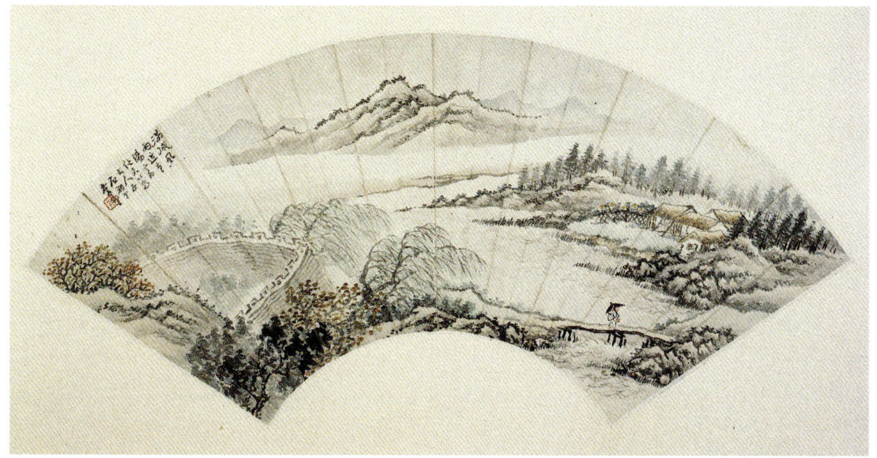

59 NIE OU 聶鷗
1948–

Reading

INK AND SLIGHT COLOUR ON PAPER
SQUARE PAINTING IN WESTERN MOUNT,
FRAMED, 66.6 × 66.2 CM

EA 1995.223

Inscribed: 聶鷗作讀書圖於秋日
Picture of reading books Done (by) Nie Ou on an autumn day

This sparse and simple composition is typical of Nie Ou's work. She has written that during the Cultural Revolution she was sent from Beijing, where she was a student, to live in a small village in the north China plains, and that the simplicity and the hardship of life there have inspired much of her painting.

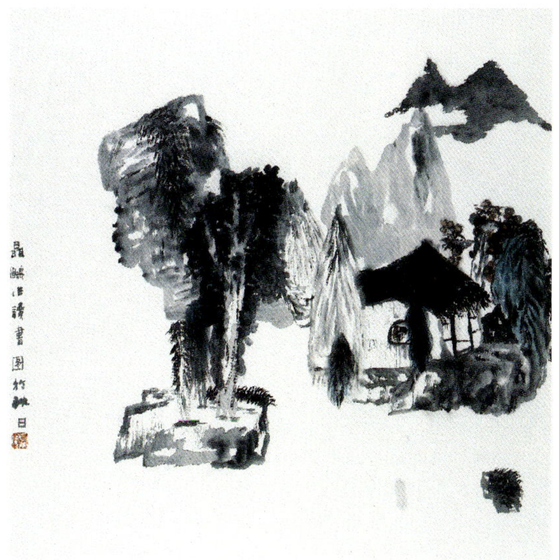

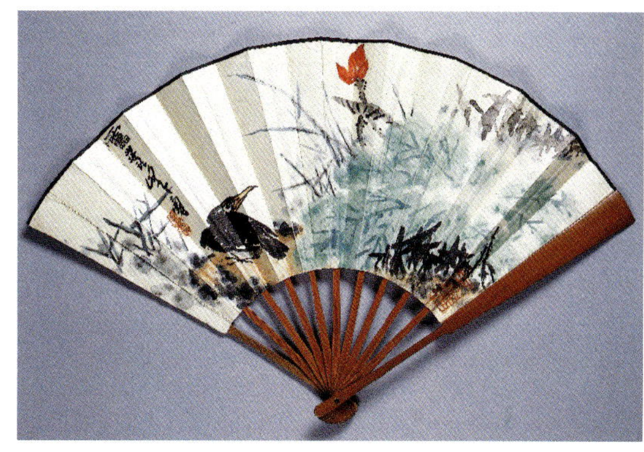

60 PAN TIANSHOU 潘天壽
1897–1971

Bird amongst plants, and calligraphy

肖似文君春鬢影，清如冰雪藐姑仙，
應 從風 格推王者，無借幽香足以傳.
錦蓉同志 ＿＿＿＿ 壬寅秋頤者壽

INK AND COLOUR ON PAPER
FOLDING FAN, L. 54 CM

EA 1995.224

Signed: 雷婆頭峰 壽者 *Leipotoufeng Shou zhe*

Pan Tianshou was a teacher and art historian, and one of the leading traditional painters of the twentieth century. He is a particularly distinguished painter of bird and flower subjects, and the vivid crow in this painting is typical of his style. The calligraphy on the reverse comprises a four-line poem followed by the inscription *Painted for Miss Jin Rong, autumn 1962 (by) Yizhe Shou.*

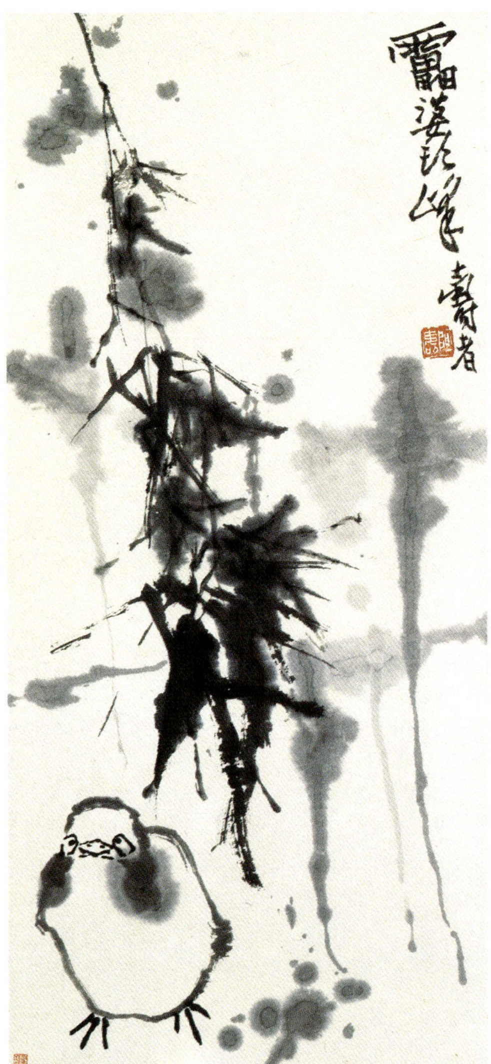

61

61   PAN TIANSHOU 潘天壽
1897–1971

Chick and bamboo

INK ON PAPER
HANGING SCROLL, FRAMED, 54.5 × 25 CM
EA 1995.225
Signed: 雷婆頭峰　壽者　　*Leipotoufeng Shouzhe*

Pan Tianshou was a follower of Wu Changshuo
(1844–1927) and his brushwork style derives from
the strong, square forms of Han (206 BC–AD 220)
dynasty clerical script. This chick appears in several
works by the artist; the use of wet ink soaking into
the paper to produce a soft, almost blotted effect is
a modern technique often used by Pan Tianshou
when painting bamboo and other plants.

62   PENG XIANCHENG 彭先誠
1941–

The Beauties' Spring Outing
春風得意麗人行

INK AND COLOUR ON PAPER
HANGING SCROLL, FRAMED, 120 × 58.4 CM
EA 1995.226
Inscribed: 35-character inscription followed by
辛末三春寫此贈之　彭先誠
Drawn in spring 1991, Xiancheng

This painting by the self-taught Sichuan artist Peng
Xiancheng illustrates a poem written in AD 753 by
Du Fu, in which he criticises the extravagance of the
Emperor's concubines' riding parties while the people
suffered hardships. It is painted in the "boneless" style
of Tang figure painting, comprising colour washes
with little or no underlying linear structure.

63   PU RU 溥儒
1896–1963

Landscapes

INK AND COLOURS ON PAPER
HANDSCROLL, 8.6 × 278 CM
EA 1995.227
Inscribed: 戊午孟春摹王石谷意于恭弟寒玉堂
*1918 early spring in the style of Wang Shigu in his
brother's studio Hanyu Tang*
Signed: 溥儒　　*Pu Ru*

Pu Xinyu, also known as Pu Ru, was a cousin of
the last emperor of the Qing dynasty; as such he
received a classical education and was able to study
at first hand paintings by Song, Yuan, Ming and
Qing masters. He remained in Peking until the
1940s, later moving to Taiwan where he became
the leading upholder of the classical tradition. The
brushwork in this painting is in the meticulous
gongbi style.

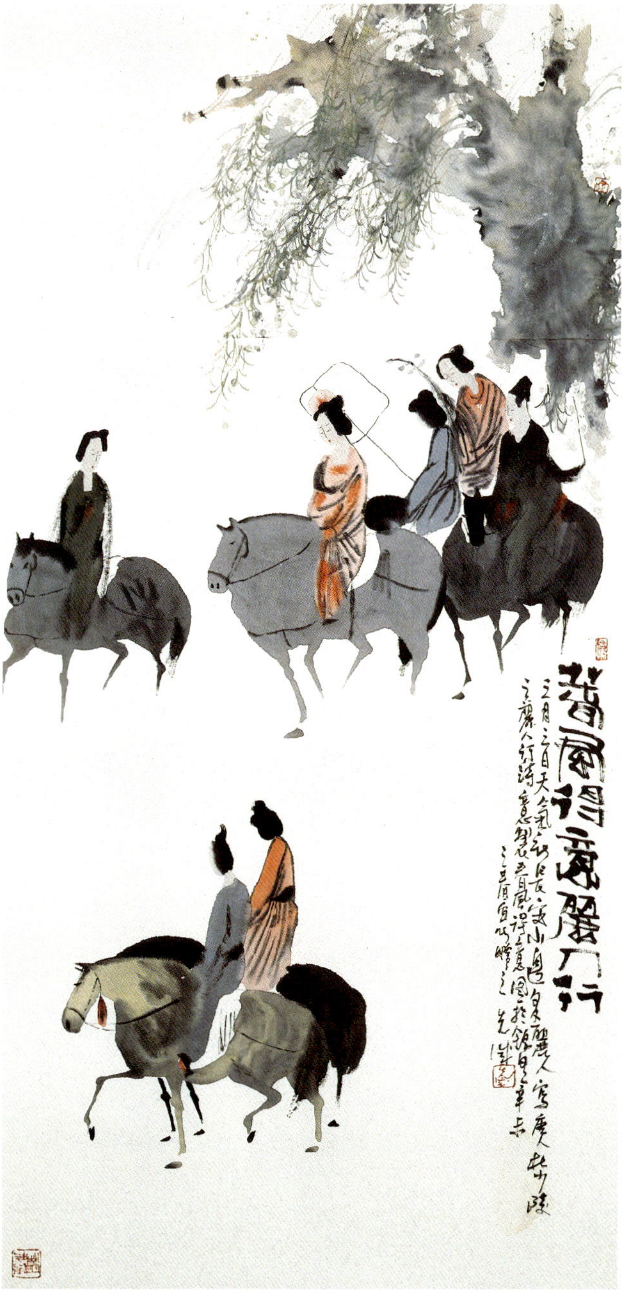

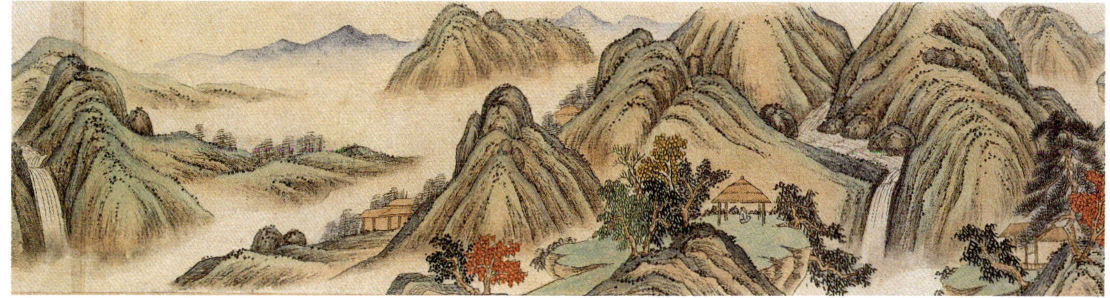

62

63 (detail)

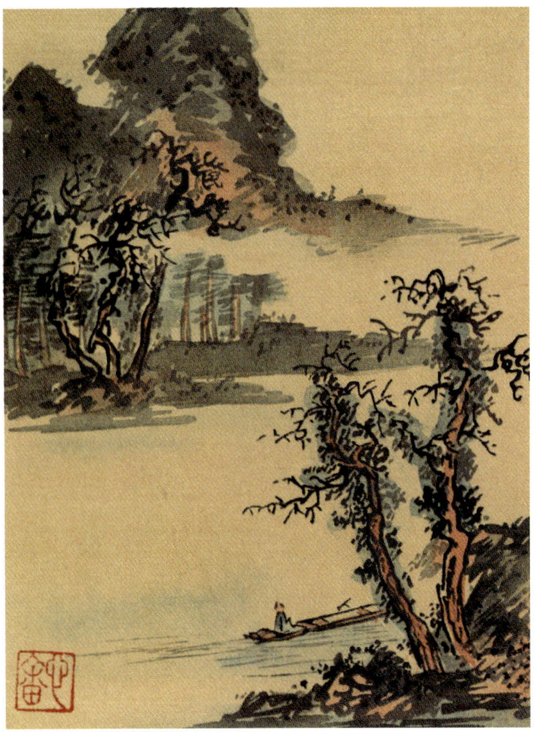

64

64 PU RU 溥儒
1896–1963

Landscapes

INK AND COLOUR ON SILK
ALBUM OF TWELVE LEAVES, EACH 17 × 13 CM
EA 1995.228
Signed: 心畬 *Xinyu*

The twelve landscapes are painted in Southern
Song (1127–1279) style and most display the
diagonally-balanced composition associated with
that period, and favoured by Pu Xinyu in his
sketches. The simplicity of the brushwork is
appropriate to the less responsive silk medium.

65 PU RU 溥儒
1896–1963

Figure in a mountain landscape

INK AND COLOUR ON PAPER
HANGING SCROLL, FRAMED, 130.5 × 41.6 CM
EA 1995.229

Inscribed: 18-character inscription ending
鳴先先生雅正 溥儒

For Mr. Ming Xian Pu Ru

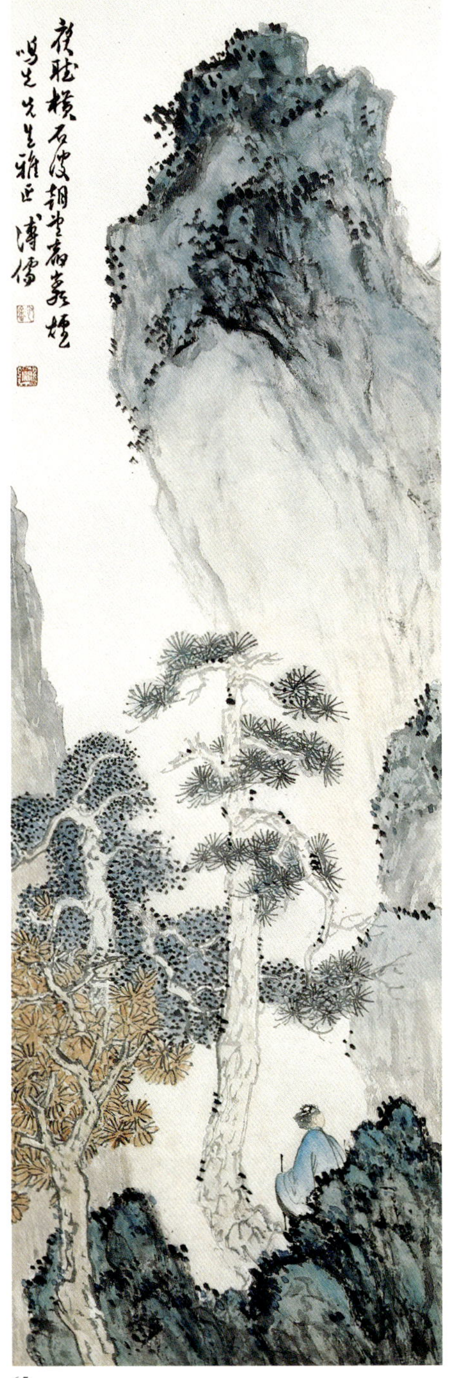

65

The subject and composition of this painting are
typical of Pu Xinyu's work but the brushwork is
quite simple and loose by his standards. It may be
compared with cat. no. 117, another painting of a
scholar in a landscape, on which Pu Xinyu
collaborated with Zhang Daqian.

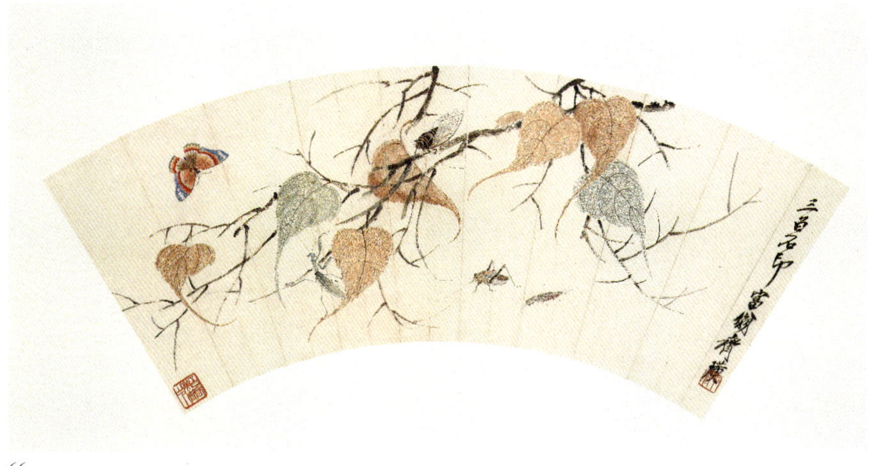

66

66 QI BAISHI 齊白石
1863–1957

Bodhi leaves and insects

INK AND COLOUR ON PAPER
FAN PAINTING, FRAMED, LENGTH 103 CM
EA 1995.230
Signed: 三百石印富翁齊璜
Sanbaidan yin fuweng Qihuang

Qi Baishi, perhaps the most renowned of all modern
Chinese painters, is particularly celebrated for his
depictions of bodhi leaves and insects, in which he
combines two contrasting styles of brushwork –
meticulous (*gongbi*) and expressive (*xieyi*).

67 QIAN SHOUTIE 錢瘦鐵
1896–1967
TANG YUN 唐雲
1910–93

Landscape and calligraphy

INK ON PAPER
FAN PAINTINGS, MOUNTED TOGETHER AND
FRAMED, L. 41.5 AND 41.7 CM
EA 1995.231 a,b
Calligraphy inscribed:
Painted for Chen Kai (by) Lao Yao 陳凱學弟屬 老藥
Landscape signed: *Qian Ya* 錢崖

Tang Yun is well-known as a collector and
connoisseur, and as an artist is entirely self-taught
(see cat.no.28). Qian Shoutie, also known as Qian
Ya, from Wuxi in Jiangsu was a traditional painter
interested in calligraphy and archaic scripts; this fan
painting incorporating hills, water, trees and
pavilions is a typically conservative ink
monochrome landscape.

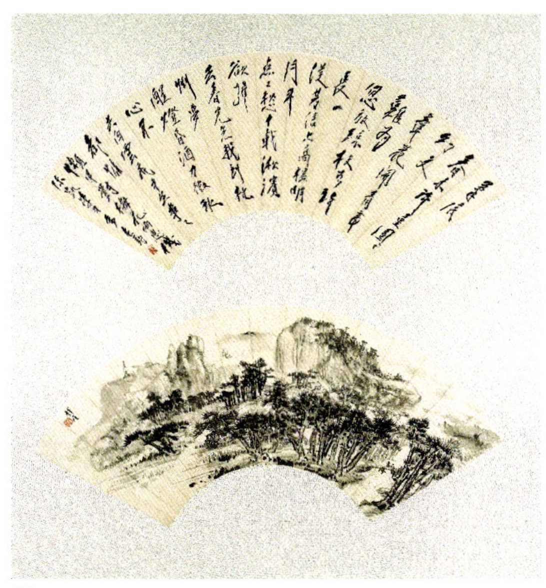

67

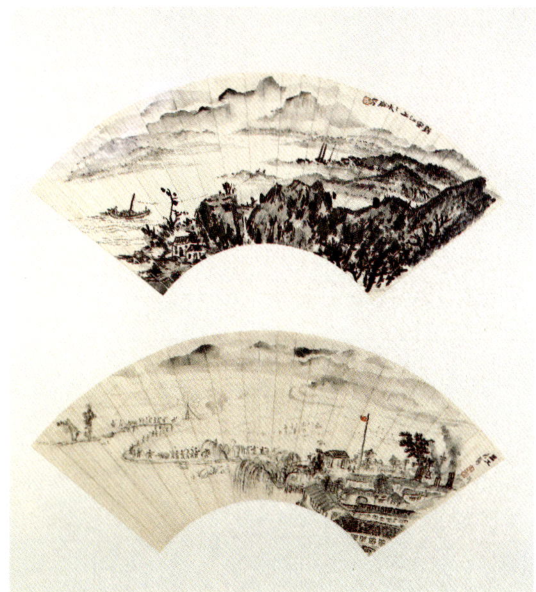

68

69 QIAN SONGYAN 錢松岩
1898–1985

River landscape

INK AND COLOUR ON PAPER
HANGING SCROLL, FRAMED
EA 1995.233

Inscribed: 江南魚米地處處繪新圖 我愛這邊好
掀髯畫太湖 錢松岩作于南京

27-character inscription ending
Done at Nanjing (by) Qian Songyan

Qian Songyan from Yixing in prosperous Jiangsu
province was a traditional landscape painter who
worked mostly in Nanjing, producing in the 1950s
and early 1960s many industrial landscapes regarded
as combining romanticism with realism. This quiet
scene represents Lake Tai in the Jiangnan (Jiangsu
and Zhejiang) region of "fish and rice" referred to
in the inscription.

68 QIAN SHOUTIE 錢瘦鐵
1896–1967

Boats on the River Xin'an and *Going
to Work* 新安江上 上水船 and 出工

INK AND INK AND COLOUR ON PAPER
FAN PAINTINGS, FRAMED, L. 50 AND 49.8 CM
EA 1995.232 a,b

(a) signed: 叔崖 *Shu Ya*

(b) signed: 瘦鐵 *Shoutie*

The depth of the landscape in Boats on the River
Xin'an is conveyed in the constrained fan format by
the distant hills across an expanse of water; in
Going to Work, the size of the fields is accentuated
by the small proportions of the figures already
labouring and the meandering of the file of figures
and animals on their way. The red flag shows this to
be a political work, probably of the 1960s, when
the filing workers occur on painted porcelain
plaques and other propaganda objects of the period.

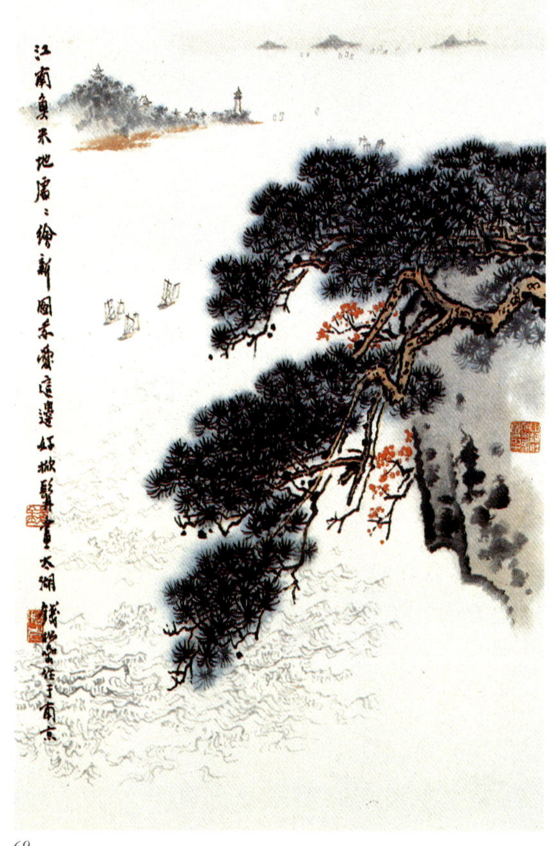

69

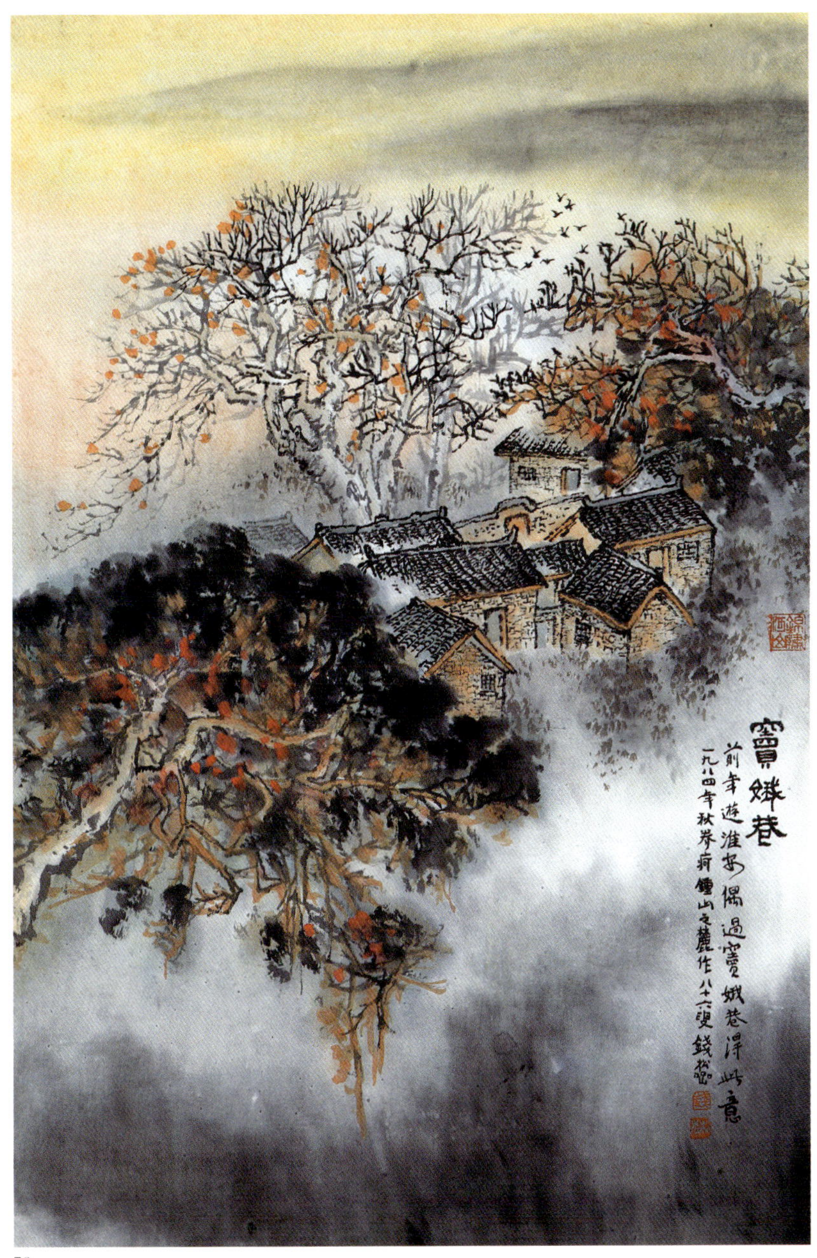

70

70 QIAN SONGYAN 錢松岩
1898–1985

Du'e Lane 寶娥巷

INK AND COLOUR ON PAPER
HANGING SCROLL IN WESTERN MOUNT,
FRAMED 67.7 × 45.2 CM

EA 1995.234

Inscribed: 前年游淮安偶過寶娥巷得此意
一九八四年秋養痾鍾山之麓作八十六叟　錢松岩
36-character inscription ending
Old gentleman of eighty-six, Qian Songyan

Du'E Lane is a place the artist had passed by in Huai'an, Jiangsu, the year before painting this landscape. Qian Songyan was a traditional Chinese painter yet the many twentieth-century features of this landscape include the high view, the detail of the bricks and the use of bright colour, particularly in the coloured washes of the background.

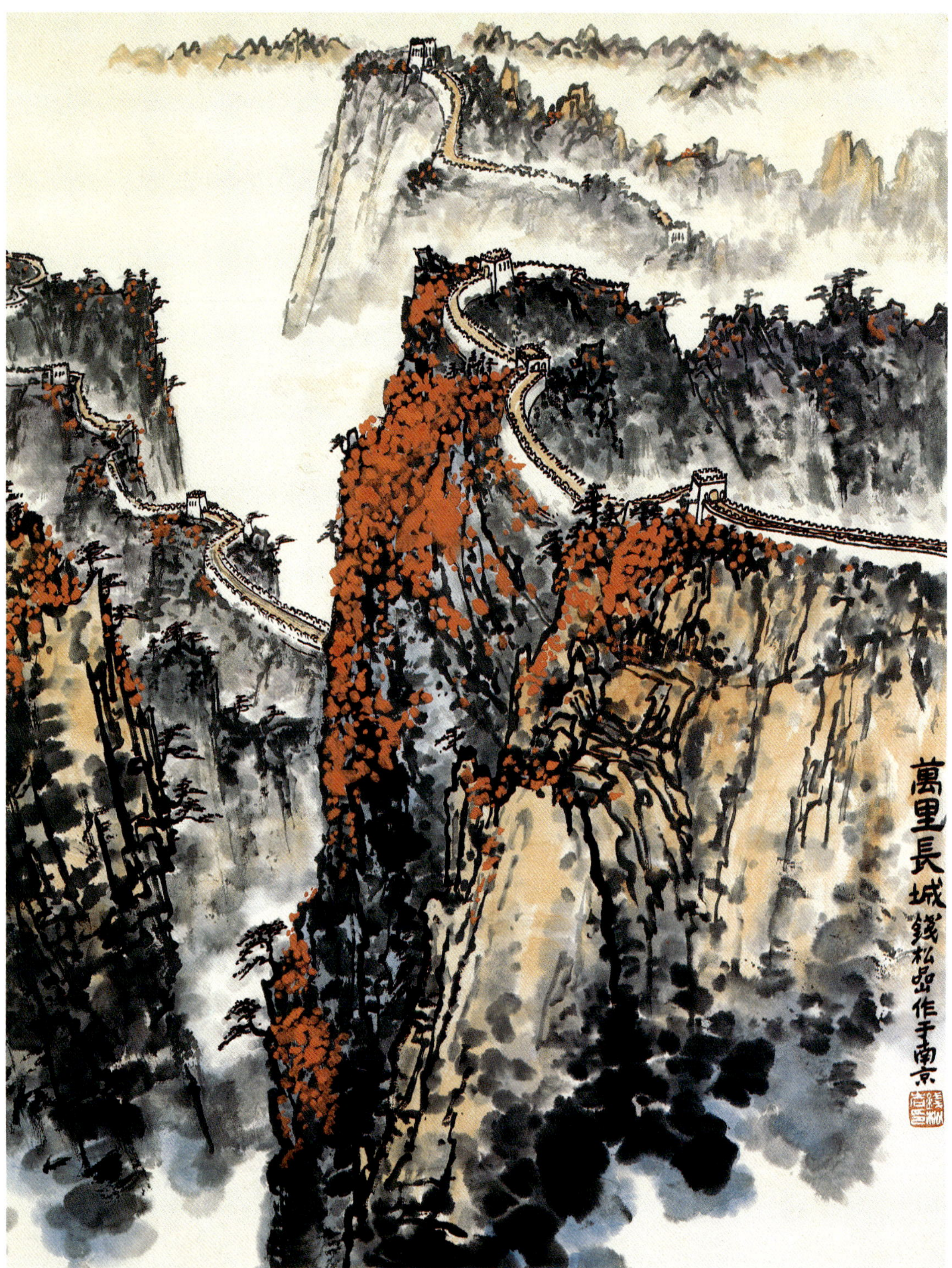

71

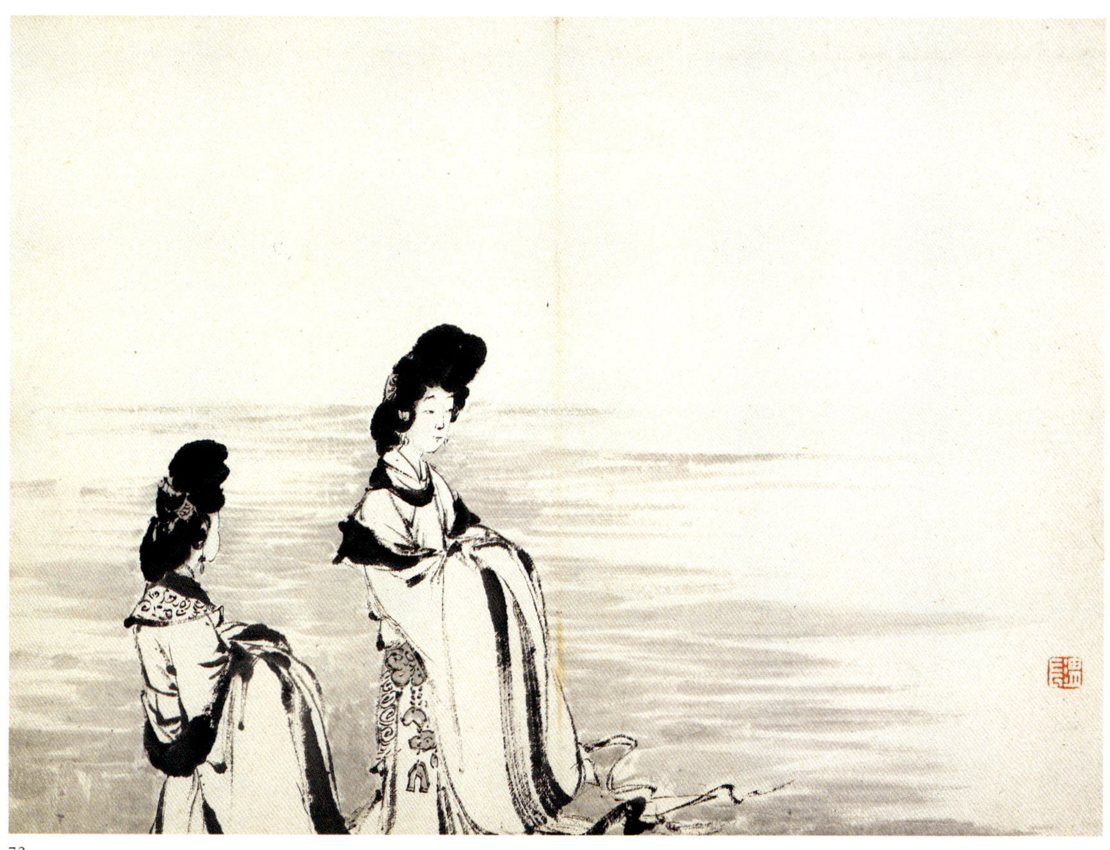

72

72 REN XIONG 任熊
1820–57

Various subjects

INK AND INK AND COLOUR ON PAPER
ALBUM OF EIGHTEEN LEAVES AND ONE LEAF
CALLIGRAPHY, EACH 29.3 41 CM
EA 1995.236 a–s
Variously inscribed

Ren Xiong was a versatile artist who excelled in
the combination of the traditional and the popular
with which the Shanghai School, in which he was
active, is associated. This album includes landscapes,
figures, and bird and flower paintings; the leaf
illustrated here depicts in a restrained fashion the
usually colourful and decoratively painted subject of
female figures.

71 QIAN SONGYAN 錢松岩
1898–1985

Great Wall landscape

INK AND COLOUR ON PAPER
HANGING SCROLL, FRAMED, 67.5 × 51.7 CM
EA 1995.235
Inscribed: 萬里長城 錢松岩作于南京
*The Great Wall, painted (by) Qian Songyan at
Nanjing*

Qian Songyan was the foremost of artists using red
in paintings of the 1960s as an allusion to Mao
Zedong and the Communist cause, often in works
that combined landscape with depictions of
industrial progress. The red is here applied as on
overlay of *dian* in the traditional manner.

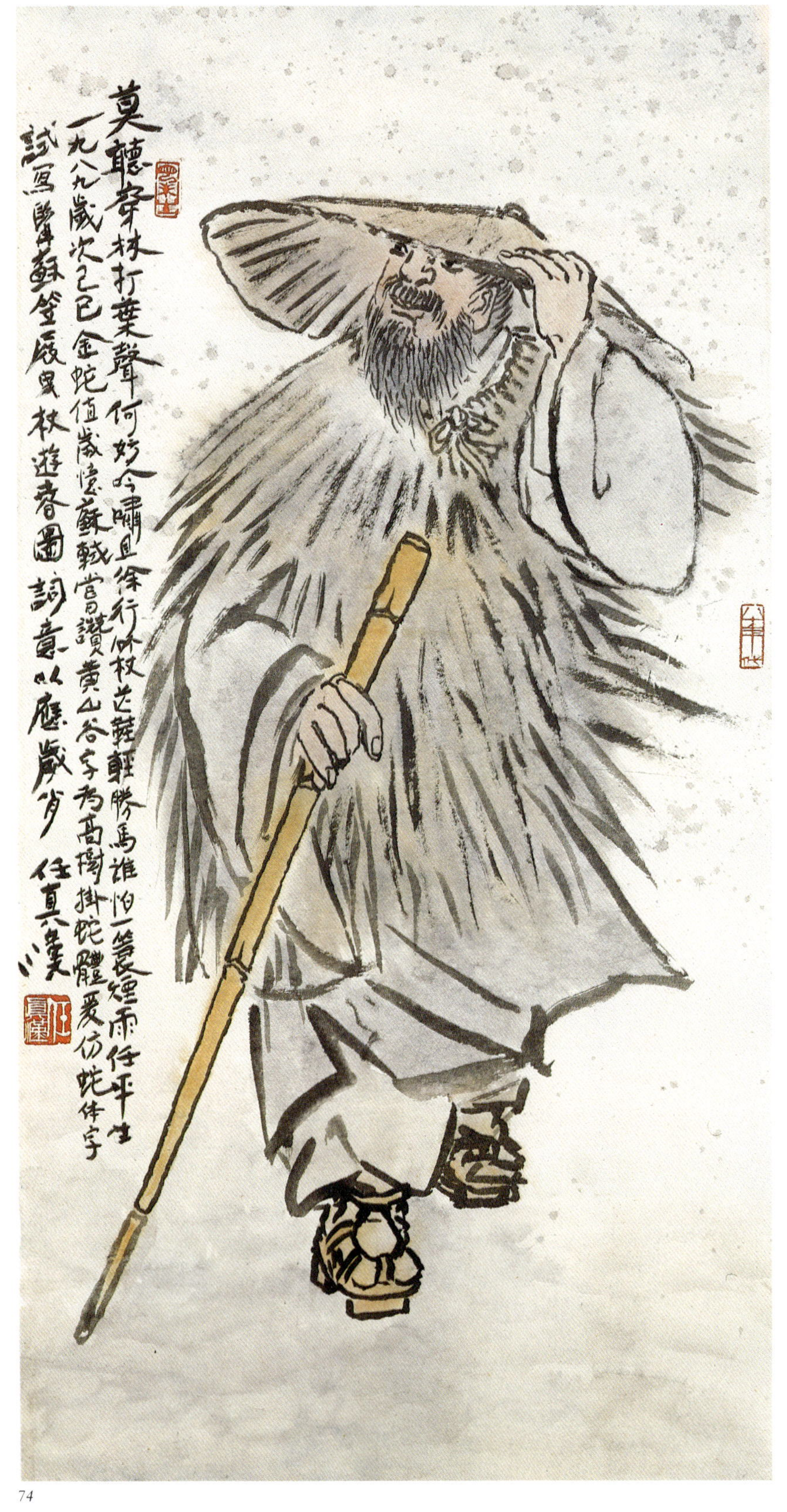

莫聽穿林打葉聲　何妨吟嘯且徐行　竹杖芒鞋輕勝馬　誰怕　一簑煙雨任平生
一九八九歲次己巳金蛇值歲憶蘇軾嘗曰讚黃山谷字為高樹掛蛇體愛仿蛇体字
試寫聲聲蘇笙殘杖遊春圖詞意以應歲歲　任真漢

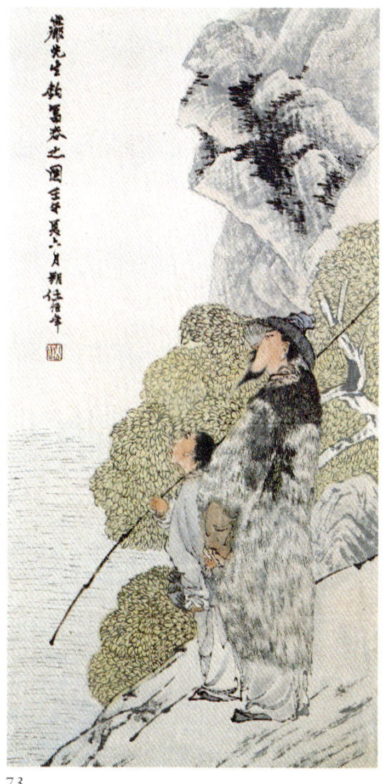

73

73 After REN YI 任頤
1840–95

Yan Ziling fishing in Spring

INK AND COLOUR ON PAPER
HANGING SCROLL, FRAMED, 99 × 48.5 CM
EA 1995.237

Inscribed: 岩先生鉤富春之圖 壬午夏六月朔 任伯年
*Mr. Yan fishing in spring 1882 summer 6th month
Ren Bonian*

This painting is a competent copy after Ren Yi, also
known as Ren Bonian, who was a leading Shanghai
School painter. It depicts the Eastern Han
(AD 25–220) dynasty hermit Yan Ziling on a fishing
expedition, and may be compared with a similar
composition now in the Palace Museum, Beijing.

74 REN ZHENHAN 任眞漢
1907–1991?

The poet Su Dongpo (1037–1101)

INK AND COLOUR ON PAPER
HANGING SCROLL, FRAMED. 94 × 48.6 CM
EA 1995.238

Published: *Zhongguo dangdai guohuajia cidian*,
Hangzhou, 1990, p.659

Inscribed: 一九八九歲次己巳金蛇值歲憶蘇軾譽讚黃山谷
字爲高樹掛蛇體爰仿蛇體字試寫髯蘇笠屐曳杖
游春圖詞意以應歲旨
48-character inscription followed by signature:
任眞漢　　*Ren Zhenhan*

Su Dongpo, also known as Su Shi, was one of the
greatest calligraphers and poets of the Northern
Song (960–1127) dynasty. Ren Zhenhan here
depicts him in the image of his own poem –
carrying a stick, dressed in hermit's clothes – and in
the specific brushwork style termed by Su Shi when
describing the calligraphy of his contemporary
Huang Tingjian (1045–1105) as "snake hanging
from a tree". The painting is dated 1989, the year
of the snake. Ren favoured literary subjects for his
figure paintings; this scroll may be compared with
Shanghai School figures of the 19th century.

75 REN ZHENHAN 任眞漢
1907–1991?

Landscape

INK AND SLIGHT COLOUR ON PAPER
Hanging scroll, framed, 68.2 × 53.7 cm
EA 1995.239

Inscribed: 己巳夏寫大屯積雪 眞漢幷題
69-character inscription ending
Drawn in summer 1989, snow on Datun, Zhenhan

Ren Zhenhan, from Canton, lived while young in
Taiwan, Japan and Hong Kong as well as on the
mainland. He specialised in oil painting, only
returning to traditional painting in the 1950s. This
powerful landscape, which probably depicts a
mountain in northern Taiwan, is freely executed in
traditional materials.

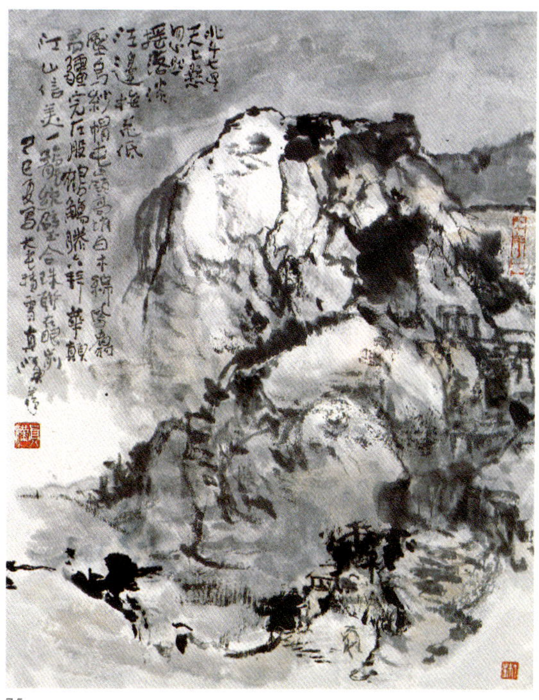

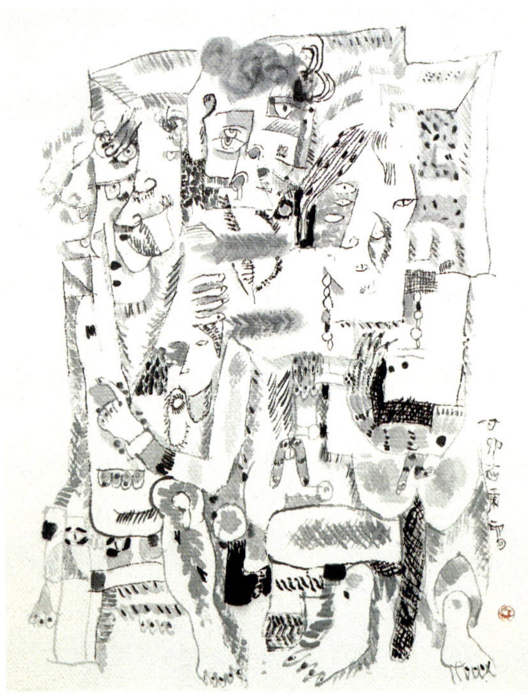

76

76   SHI HU 石虎
1942–

Figure

INK ON PAPER

HANGING SCROLL, FRAMED, 94.3 × 76.2 CM

EA 1995.240

Signed: 石虎   *Shi Hu, 1987*

Shi Hu, whose name means "Stone Tiger", trained
in Beijing and Hangzhou and now lives in Macau.
He has travelled extensively in Africa. The
calligraphy on this painting is idiosyncratic and the
seal combines the character *shi* with a picture of a
tiger (*hu*) copied from Han (206 BC–AD 220)
dynasty architectural ornament.

77   SHI HU 石虎
1942–

Nudes

INK ON PAPER

PAINTING IN WESTERN MOUNT, FRAMED,
38.8 × 28.5 CM

EA 1995.241

Inscribed:
28-character inscription followed by signature

石虎   *Shi Hu*

Shi Hu here combines figure drawing in western
style with a background of Chinese ink painting, in
an original synthesis of two traditions. His recent
works are executed in bright colours rather than
ink monochrome.

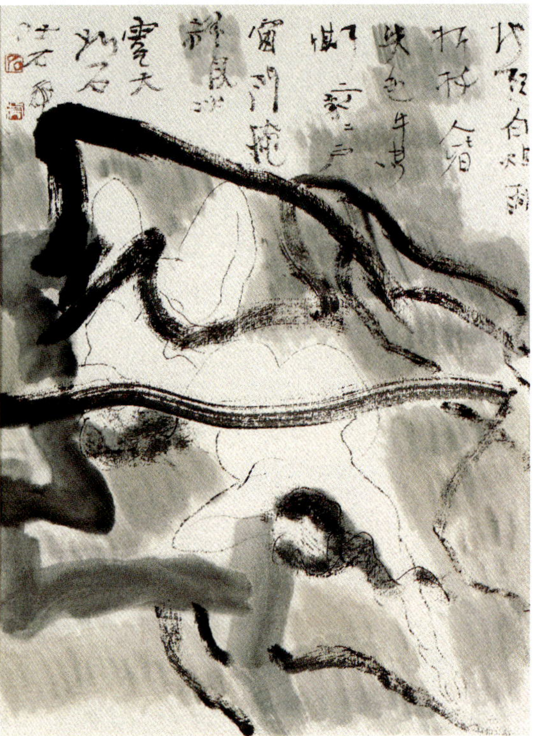

77

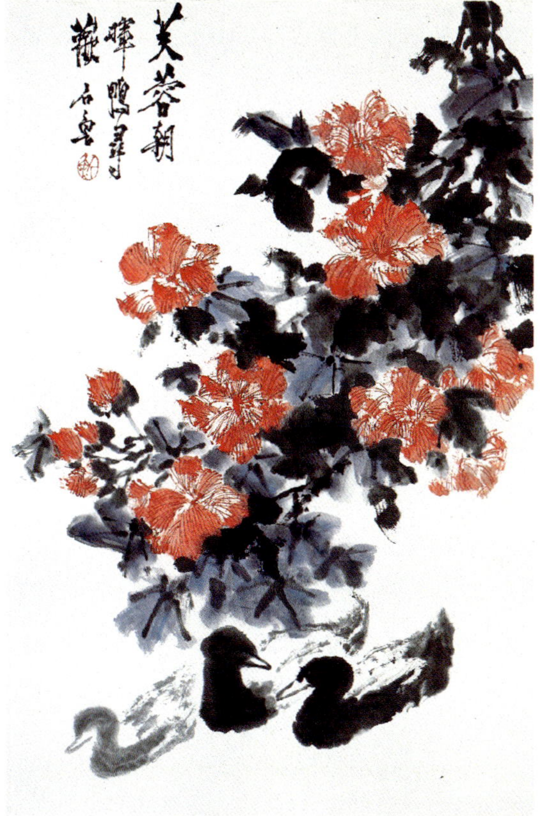

78 SHI LU 石魯
1919–82

Hibiscus and ducks

INK AND COLOUR ON PAPER

HANGING SCROLL, 99 × 67 CM

EA 1995.242

Inscribed: 芙蓉朝暉鴨尋歡 石魯
*Ducks pleasure-seeking amongst hibiscus in the
morning sunshine Shi Lu*

Shi Lu took up his name at the age of 21 from the
17th-century painter Shi Tao and the 20th-century
socialist Lu Xun, having renounced his landowning
literati background. His reputation as an artist is
that of eccentric genius. Many of his paintings,
particularly those on rustic themes, are in the black
and red colours seen here; the palette subsequently
acquired political symbolism, and was used for
landscapes by many artists in the early 1960s.

79 SHI LU 石魯
1919–82

Landscape

INK ON PAPER

HANGING SCROLL, FRAMED, 136 × 68 CM

EA 1995.243

Inscribed: 華嶽　顛渺＿＿　石魯寫于長安
*Peaks on Mount Hua…Drawn by Shi Lu at
Chang'an*

Ink monochrome paintings are central to the
Chinese landscape tradition but the exclusive use of
ink in such a large, simplified landscape is striking,
and its density is varied to great effect. In the early
1970s Shi Lu painted several landscapes of Mount
Hua in Shaanxi province, one of China's great
mountains; Chang'an is the classical name for Xi'an
in the same province, where Shi Lu was a leading
member of the group of painters known as the Xi'an
School.

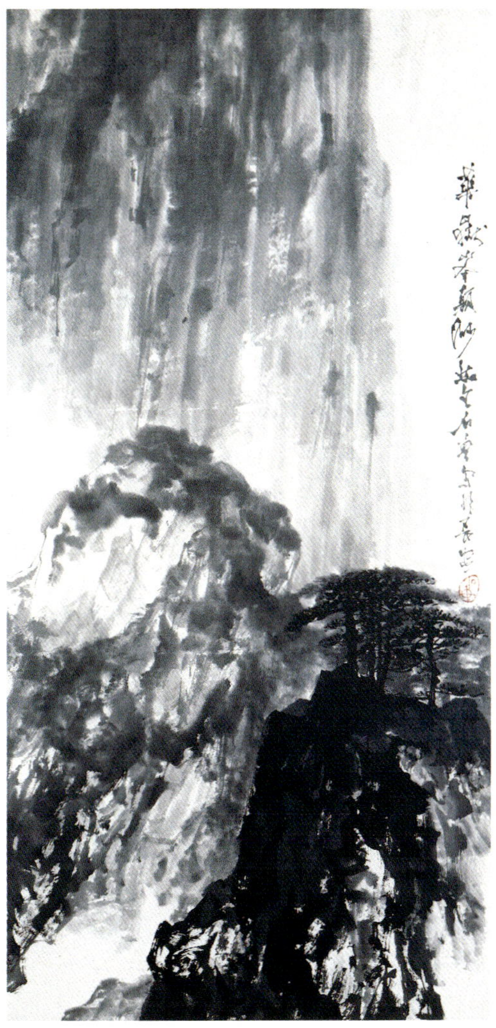

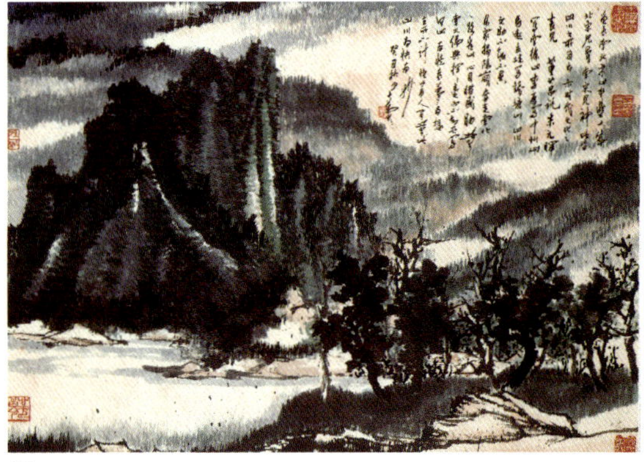

80

80 SHIWAN SHANREN 十萬山人 (SUN XINGGE 孫星閣) 1897–

Landscape

INK AND COLOUR ON PAPER
HORIZONTAL SCROLL IN WESTERN MOUNT,
FRAMED, 58 × 84 CM
EA 1995.244
Inscribed: 128-character inscription ending
癸丑秋月 十萬山人
1973, autumn, Shiwan shanren

The long inscription refers to the great Northern Song (960–1127) calligraphers and the late Ming painting theorist Dong Qichang (1555–1636), and indicates that this is a landscape in Sichuan province. The darkness and contours of the hills are reminiscent of the paintings of Gong Xian (1619–89), while the short repeated vertical and horizontal brushstrokes reinforce the formulaic aspects of the painting.

81 SONG WENZHI 宋文治 1919–

Landscape

INK AND SLIGHT COLOUR ON PAPER
HANGING SCROLL, FRAMED, 128.5 × 66.2 CM
EA 1995.245
Inscribed: 八一年夏文治寫於南京
Painted at Nanjing (by) Wenzhi, summer 1981

Song Wenzhi is a largely self-taught artist influenced by Wu Hufan and subsequently by Fu Baoshi. The modern compositional device of a long view across mountain peaks is one favoured, and used to good effect, by this artist. The landscape depicts Mount Huang in Anhui province not far from Nanjing, where this was painted.

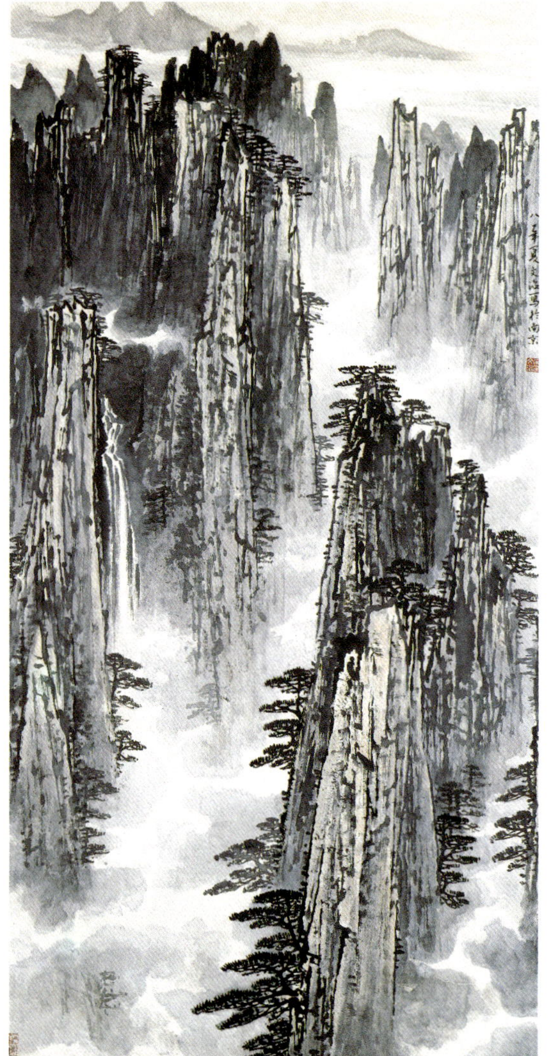

81

82 SONG WENZHI 宋文治 1919–

Mountain Waterfall Among Breezy Pines 松風潤泉圖

INK ON PAPER
VERTICAL PAINTING IN WESTERN MOUNT,
FRAMED, 69 × 44.7 CM
EA 1995.246
Inscribed: 34 characters followed by 婁江文治於金陵
Loujiang Wenzhi at Nanjing

The inscription describes a visit the artist made in 1963 to Mount Lu in Jiangxi province, which provided the inspiration for this painting. The very dark ink as it appears on the pine trees in the foreground is typical of Song Wenzhi's work, as are the strong diagonals in the composition.

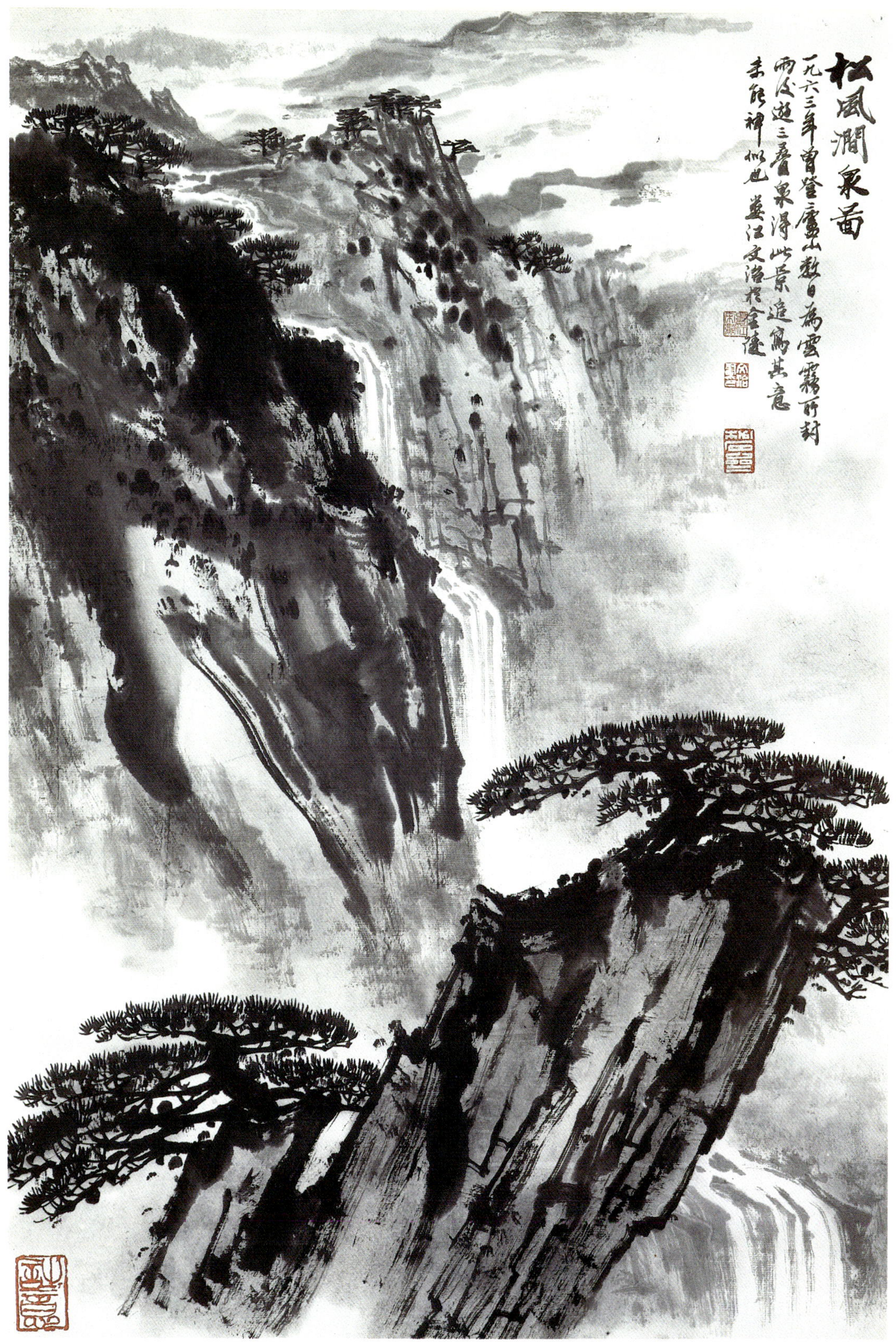

82

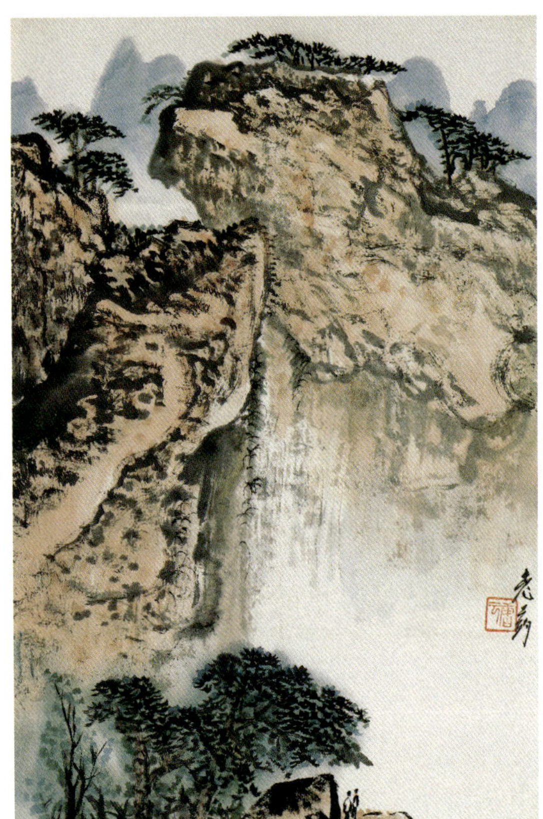

83

83 TANG YUN 唐雲
1910–93

Landscape

INK AND COLOUR ON PAPER
HANGING SCROLL, FRAMED, 34 × 23 CM
EA 1995.247
Signed: 老藥 *Lao Yao*

Tang Yun (see cat.nos.28,67) from Zhejiang province is a largely self-taught painter whose style is based on the 17th and 18th century painters Shi Tao and Hua Yan. In this traditional landscape the grandeur of the view is preserved in spite of the small size of the painting.

84 WANG GEYI 王個簃
1896–

Flowers

INK AND COLOUR ON PAPER
ALBUM OF ELEVEN LEAVES, EACH 28 × 20 CM
EA 1995.250 a–k
Various inscriptions

Wang Geyi was a pupil of the Shanghai School painter Wu Changshuo (1844–1927), whose influence can be seen in this album of eleven boldly-executed flower paintings. The leaf illustrated here is inscribed with couplets about chrysanthemums, and signed *Geyi Wang Xian*.

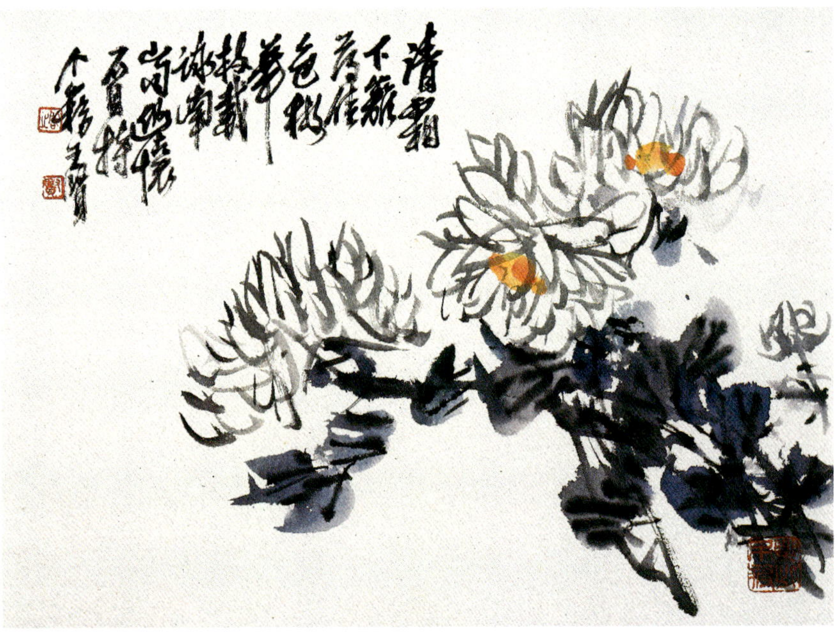

84

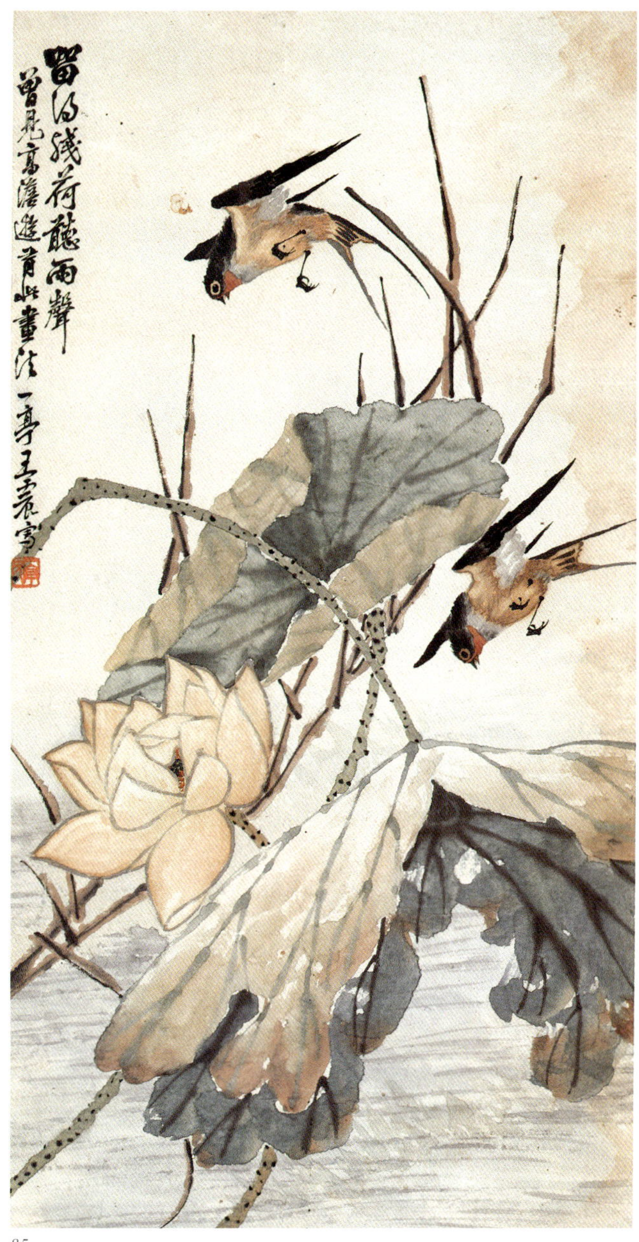

85

85 WANG YITING 王一亭
1867–1938

Listening to Rain after the Lotus has Withered 留得殘荷聽雨聲

INK AND COLOUR ON PAPER
HANGING SCROLL, 69 × 35.5 CM
EA 1995.251

Inscribed: 曾見高澹游有此書法 一亭王震寫
Yiting Wang Zhen in the style of Gao Zanyou

Wang Yiting, also known as Wang Zhen, was a pupil of the Shanghai School master Ren Yi (1840–95), and later of Wu Changshuo, whose influence is evident in the calligraphy on this painting; its momentum and rapid execution are also aspects of his style attributable to the period after 1914 when he first met Wu Changshuo. Gao Zanyou, also known as Gao Jian (1634–1707), was a landscape painter and poet from Suzhou.

86   WEI DONG 魏東
1968–

Ming Landscape – The Duel

INK AND COLOUR ON PAPER
CIRCULAR PAINTING IN WESTERN MOUNT,
FRAMED, D.27 CM
EA 1995.292

Wei Dong from Inner Mongolia studied painting in
Beijing and after four years' formal training in
classical landscape, he introduced into his work a
dichotomy of ancient and modern. This is evident
here in the depiction of twentieth-century figures
amidst a landscape painted in Ming (1368–1644)
style.

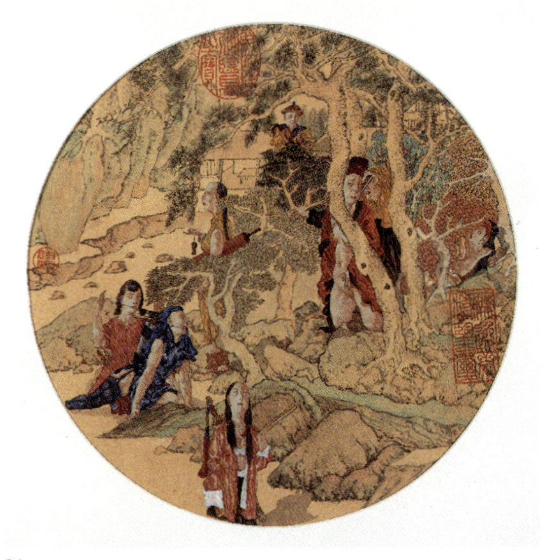

86

87   After WU GUANZHONG
吳冠中
1919–

Birds

INK AND COLOUR ON PAPER
HANGING SCROLL, FRAMED, 69 × 101 CM
EA 1995.252
Signed: 吳冠中 一九八九   *Wu Guanzhong, 1989*

This painting appears to be a copy after *Xiao niao
tian tang*, published in *Rongbaozhai huapu (44):
shanshui bufen Wu Guanzhong hui*, Hong Kong
1991, no. 11.

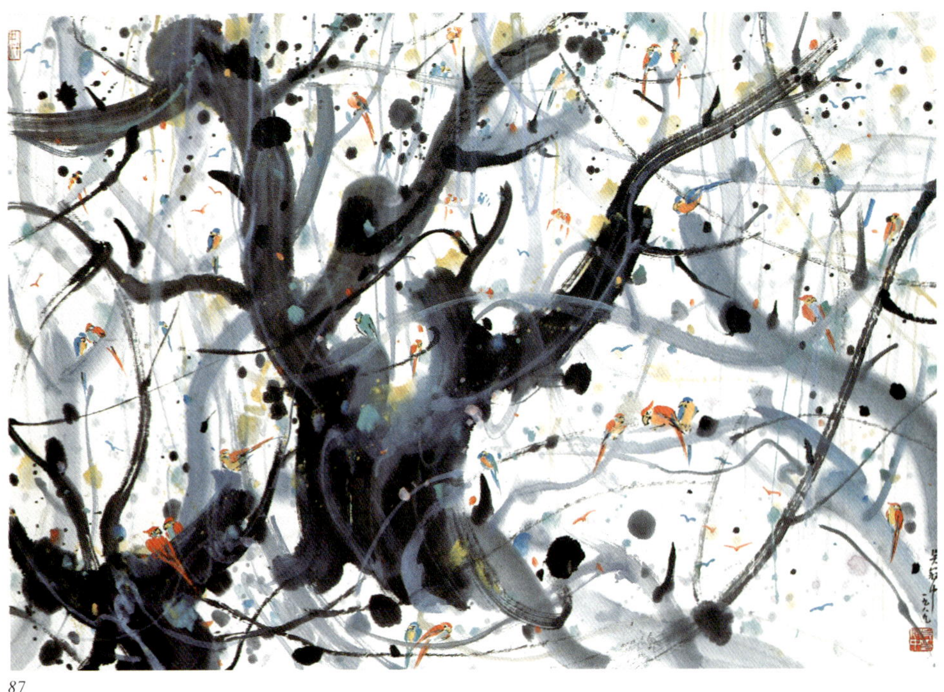

87

66

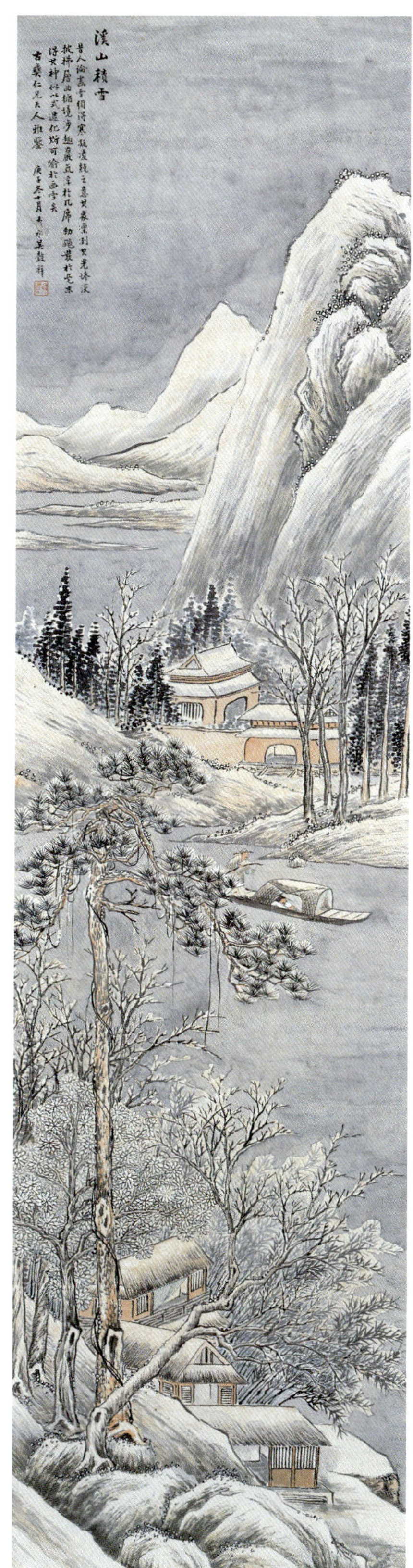

88 WU GUXIANG 吳穀祥
1848–1903

Snow on Streams and Mountains

INK AND COLOUR ON PAPER
HANGING SCROLL, FRAMED, 146 × 38.4 CM
EA 1995.253

Inscribed: 74-character inscription ending
庚子冬十月秀水 吳穀祥

1900, November, Wu Guxiang from Xiushui

Wu Guxiang, whose works are now quite rare, was
one of the leading Orthodox School painters in
Shanghai, and his landscape style derives ultimately
from the Ming masters Wen Zhengming
(1470–1559) and Tang Yin (1470–1523). He is
known to have painted sets of seasonal landscapes
and this winter scene may belong to such a group.
The inscription discusses past theories of landscape
painting.

89 WU HUFAN 吳湖帆
1894–1968

Landscapes

INK AND INK AND COLOUR ON PAPER
ALBUM OF TEN LEAVES, EACH 23.5 × 29 CM
EA 1995.254 a–j

Inscribed (1995.254 h): 竹溪隱高士 吳湖帆寫意
*Gentleman amongst bamboo and streams Wu Hufan
painting freely*

The inscription reveals that Wu Hufan painted this
scene in his own style. The remaining nine leaves of
the album are each inscribed as being painted in the
style of an early master; it is not uncommon for
albums to comprise practice works in this way.

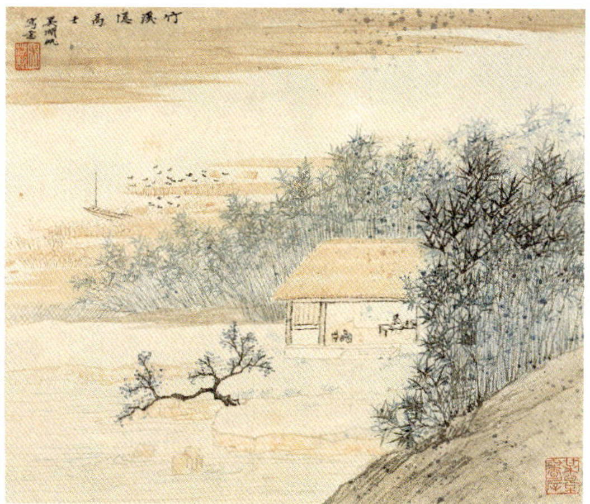

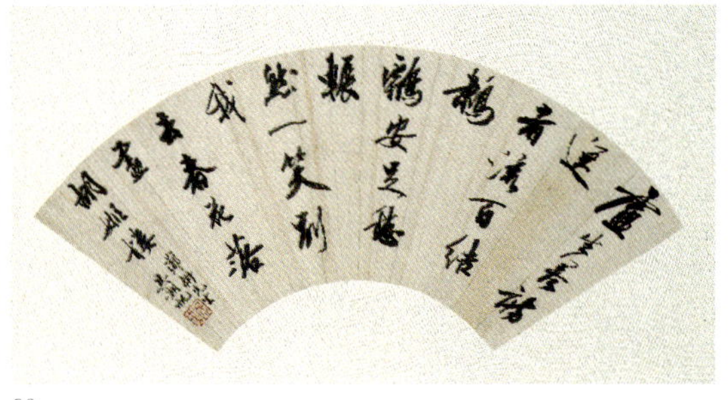

90

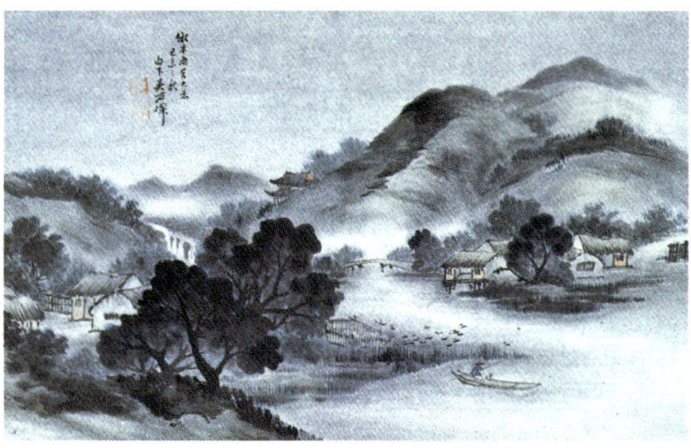

91A

90 WU HUFAN 吳湖帆
1894–1968

Calligraphy 盧生 ＿＿ ＿＿ 逸者流
百結鷦鷯安足愁　輾然
一笑別我去　春花落盡　胡姬樓

INK ON PAPER

FAN PAINTING, FRAMED, L.50.7 CM

EA 1995.290

Inscribed:
鄉耕先生吳湖帆
The rustic gentleman Wu Hufan

The calligraphy is a poem comprising four lines of
seven characters each. It is common for fans painted
on one side to bear calligraphy on the other (see
cat. no. 60). Wu Hufan was one of the most highly
educated traditional painters in Shanghai and his
large private collection of early paintings was well-
known.

91B

91 WU SHIXIAN 吳石仙
d.1917

Two landscapes

INK ON PAPER

ALBUM LEAVES MOUNTED AS HANGING
SCROLL, EACH 29 × 48 CM

EA 1995.255 a,b

Inscribed:
山色模糊新雨多　仿米襄筆法 石仙
a) *The mountain colours blurred in the fresh rain
Brushwork after Mi (Fu) Shixian*
仿米南宮大意　己未之秋　白下吳石仙
b) *Impression of Nangong (south palace) after Mi (Fu)
Shixian*

Wu Shixian, also known as Wu Qingyun, painted
sombre landscapes in heavy ink after the styles of
the 11th-century painter Mi Fu and his fellow
native of Nanjing, the 18th-century Gong Xian.
His use of western-style chiaroscuro, evident in
both these album leaves, is usually attributed to his
having spent time in Japan.

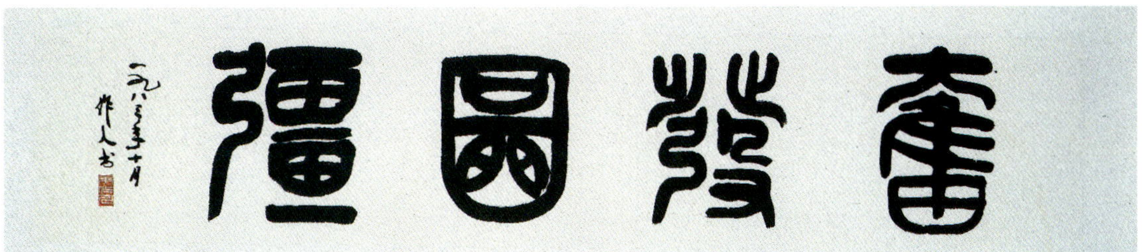

92

92 WU ZUOREN 吳作人
1908–

Calligraphy 奮發圖強

INK ON PAPER
HORIZONTAL SCROLL, FRAMED, 20 × 100.5 CM
EA 1995.256
Inscribed: 一九八三年十月 作人書
October 1983 written (by) Zuoren

Wu Zuoren was a pupil of Xu Beihong
(1898–1953) and trained in Paris and Brussels. His
western technique is always evident in his work and
he practised calligraphy chiefly to improve his
brushwork. The present example is in archaic style
and reads *fen fa tu qiang*, a four-character phrase
meaning "to go all out to make the country strong".

93 WU ZUOREN 吳作人
1908–

Outspread Wings 展翅

INK AND SLIGHT COLOUR ON PAPER
HANGING SCROLL, FRAMED, 100.4 × 52.5 CM
EA 1995.257
Signed: 一九七八年作人   *1978 Zuoren*

Wu Zuoren worked in oil and watercolour as much
as in the traditional Chinese medium until the
1970s, when he concentrated on ink paintings. His
subjects are mostly animals and he is best known
for pandas, camels, goldfish and yaks. His western
training is evident here in the predominance of ink
wash over calligraphic line.

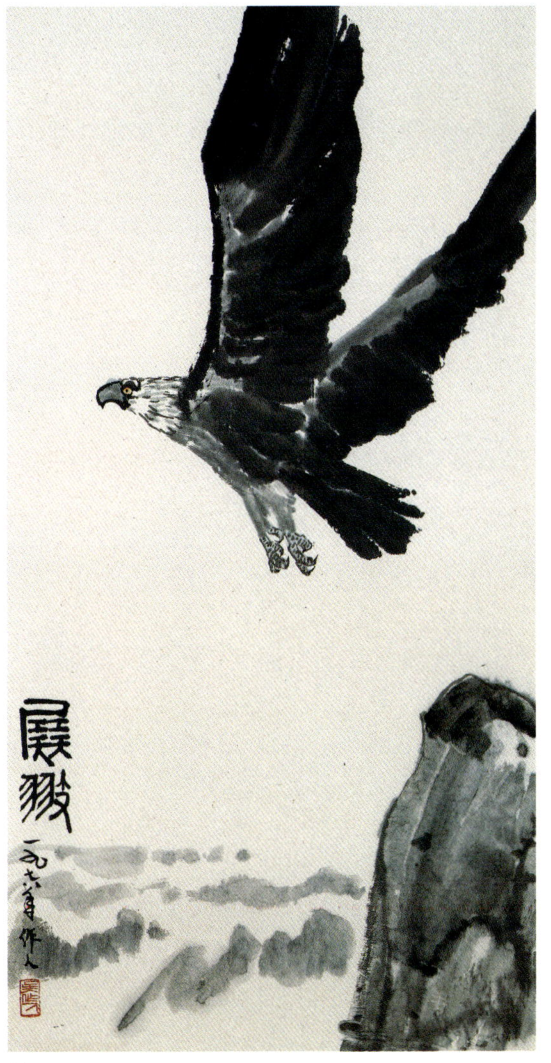

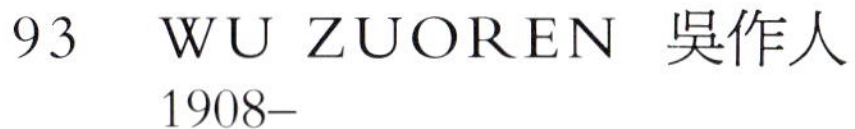

93

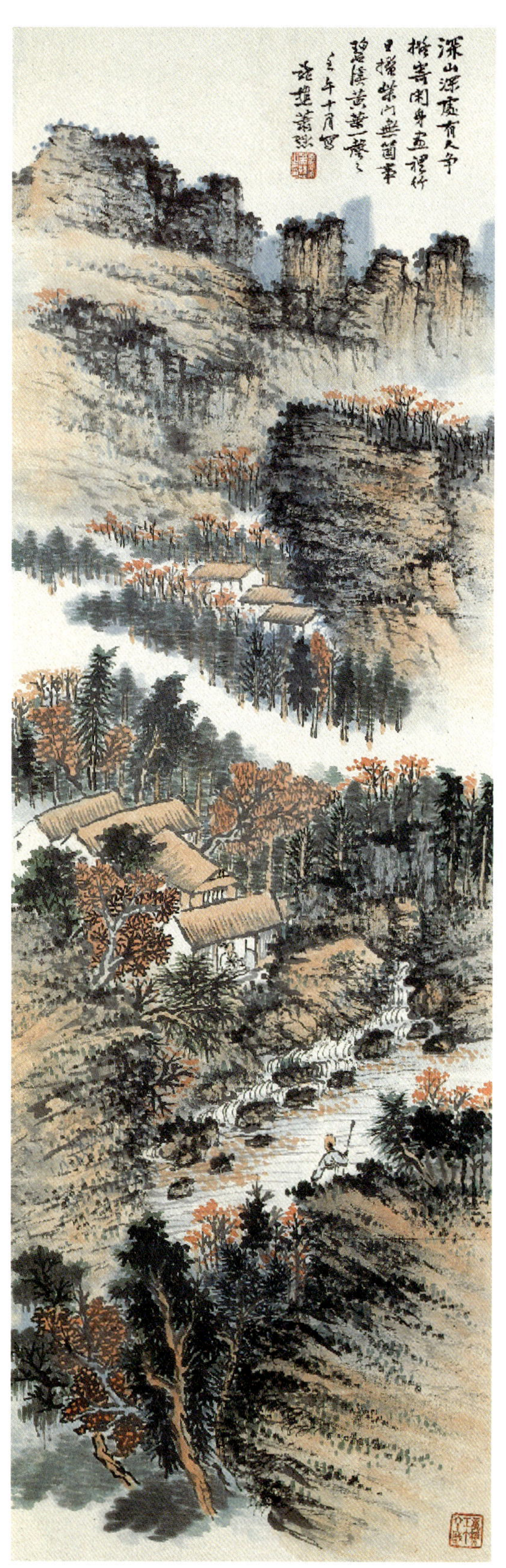

94 XIAO SUN 蕭愻
1883–1944

Landscape

INK AND COLOUR ON PAPER
HANGING SCROLL, FRAMED, 103.4 × 33.3 CM
EA 1995.258
Inscribed:
深山深處有人爭擬寄閑身畫里行日掩柴門
無個事碧溪黃葉一聲聲 壬午十月寫龍樵蕭愻

28-character poem followed by
Drawn in the tenth month of 1942 Longqiao Xiao Sun

Xiao Sun was born in Anhui province but was active in Peking as a member of the art association founded by Chen Hengke and Chen Shaomei. His dense landscape compositions derive fom late Ming painting and often include coloured texture strokes as well as colour washes.

95 XIE ZHIGUANG 謝之光
1900–76

Peony

INK AND COLOUR ON PAPER
HANGING SCROLL, 147 × 69 CM
EA 1995.259
Inscribed: 七十四歲之光
74-year-old Zhiguang

Xie Zhiguang from Yuyao, Zhejing province, is known for his bold, fluid painting style, inspired by Ren Yi (1840–95) and Qi Baishi (1863–1957). The startling pink and yellow of the peony is emphasized by the use of ink with classical buff and light blue in the rest of the painting.

94

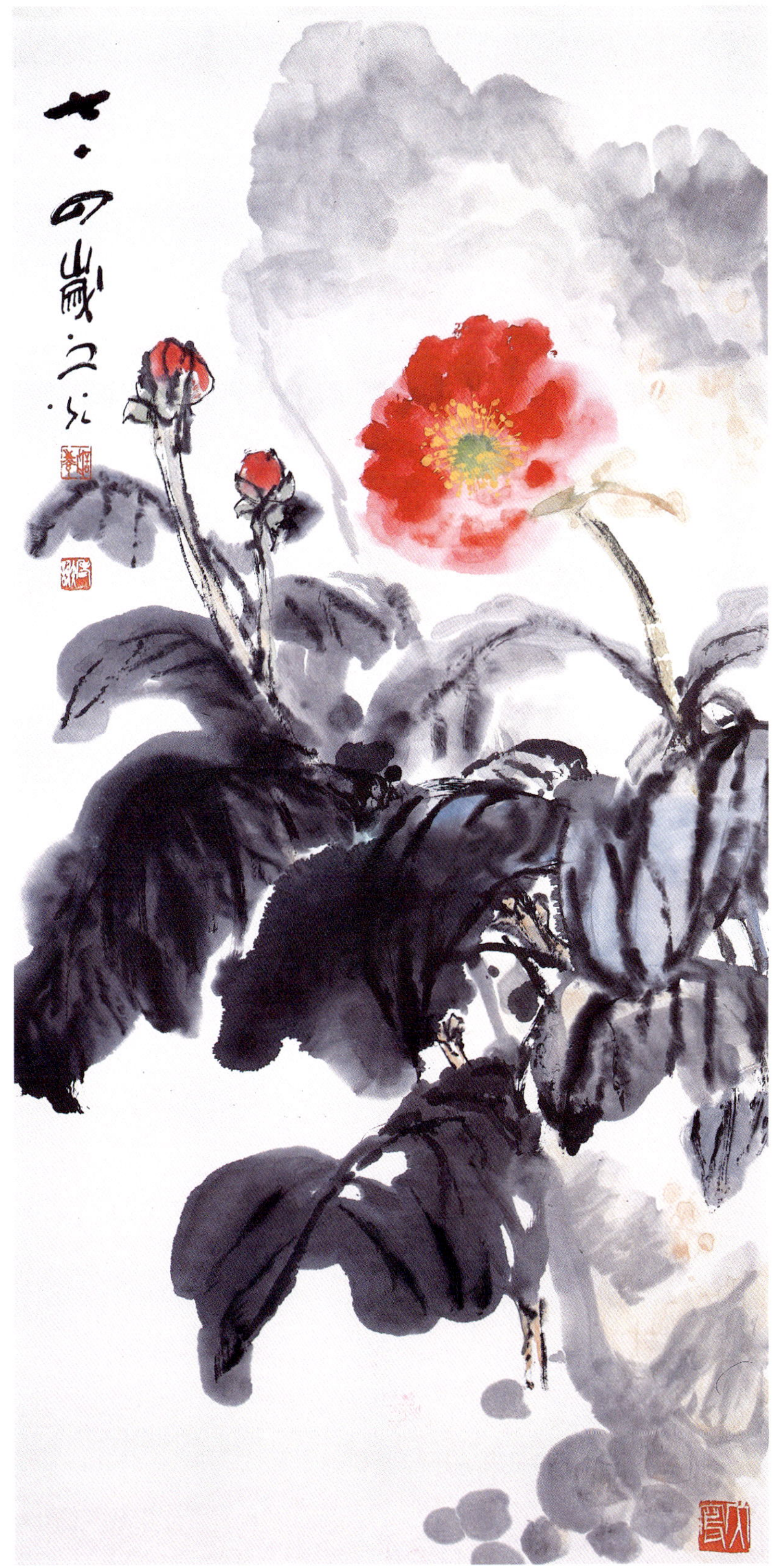

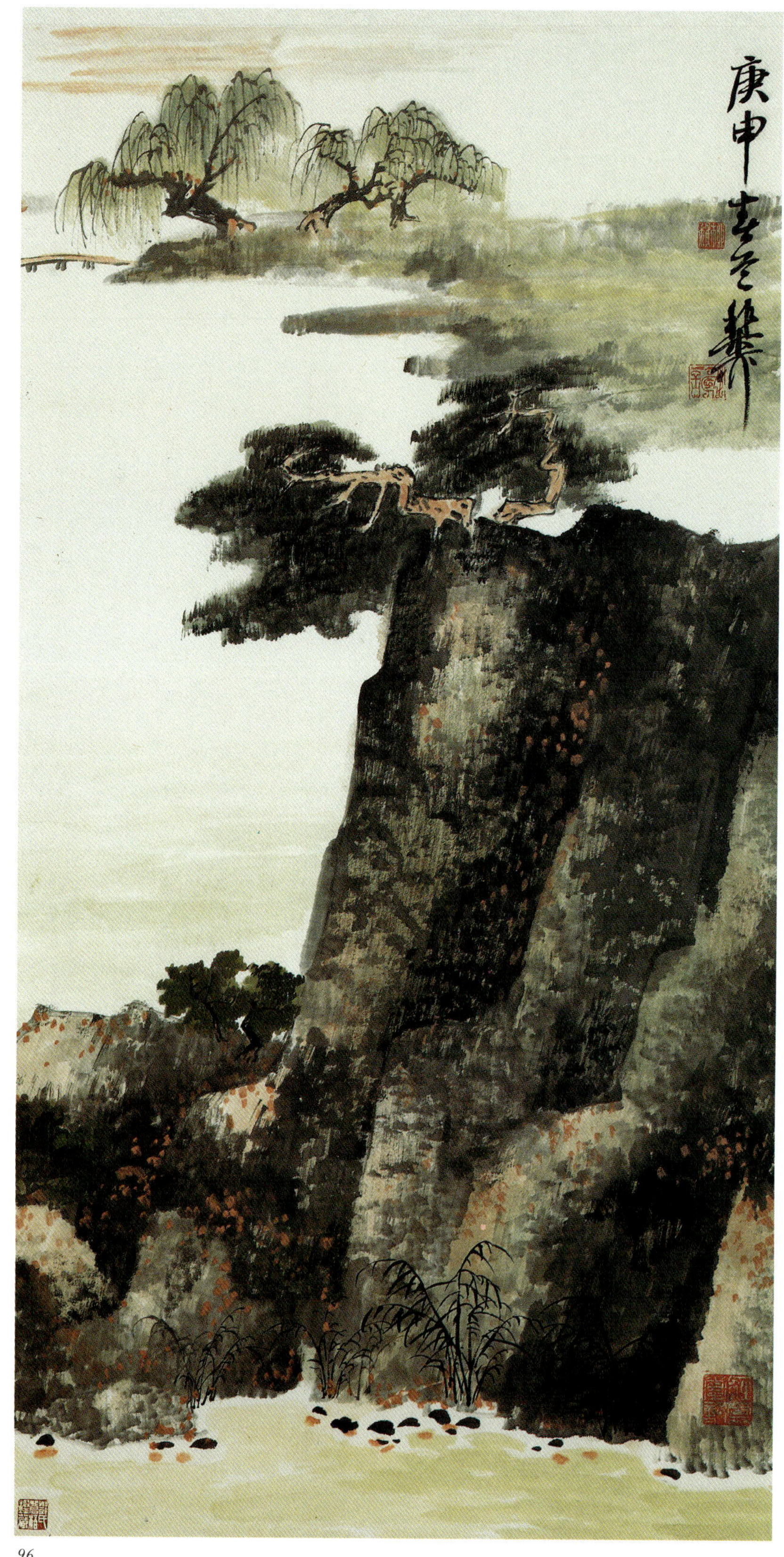

庚申春三月 藝

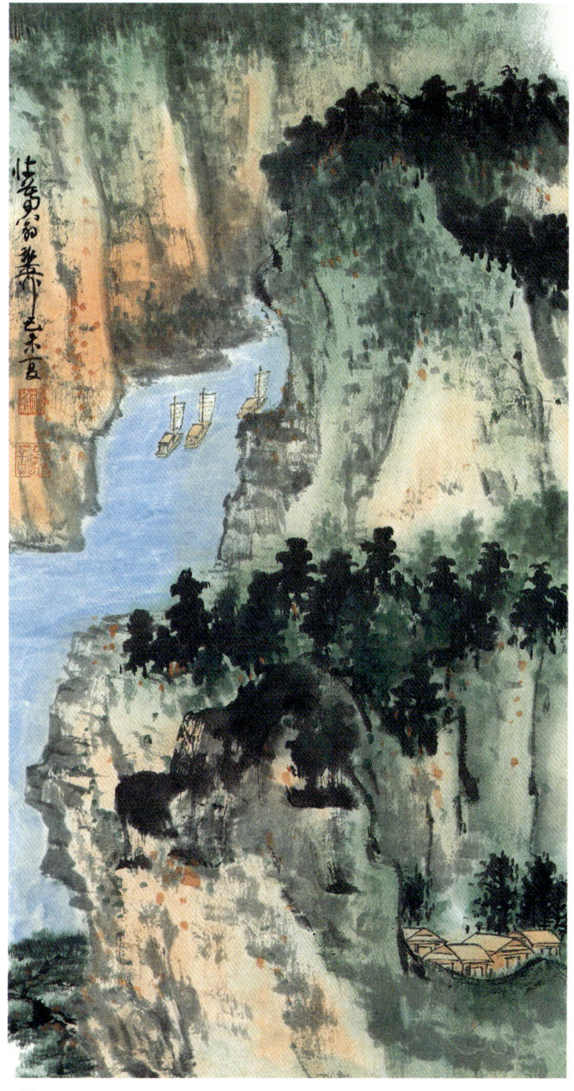
97

96 XIE ZHILIU 謝稚柳
1910–

Landscape

INK AND COLOUR ON PAPER
HANGING SCROLL, FRAMED, 102 × 52 CM
EA 1995.260
Inscribed: 庚申春盡 謝稚柳
Spring 1980, Xie Zhiliu

Xie Zhiliu is a landscape painter from Jiangsu, a
connoisseur who has written extensively on the
masters of the Northern Song (960–1127) dynasty.
His own landscapes make extensive use of colour
within the classical limits of blue, green and buff
pigments which he sometimes brightened by
mixing with foreign watercolours.

97 XIE ZHILIU 謝稚柳
1910–

Landscape

INK AND COLOUR ON PAPER
HANGING SCROLL, FRAMED. 66.6 × 34.6 CM
EA 1995.261
Inscribed: ＿＿ 翁謝稚柳己未夏
＿ ＿ old gentleman Xie Zhiliu, summer 1979

This composition, in which boats on a river are
viewed from above a gorge, is a recurrent one in
guohua painting of the mid-twentieth century. Xie
Zhiliu uses intensified classical colours throughout,
even for some of the *dian* (dots) which are generally
added in ink, also seen here, to accentuate the
forms of the landscape.

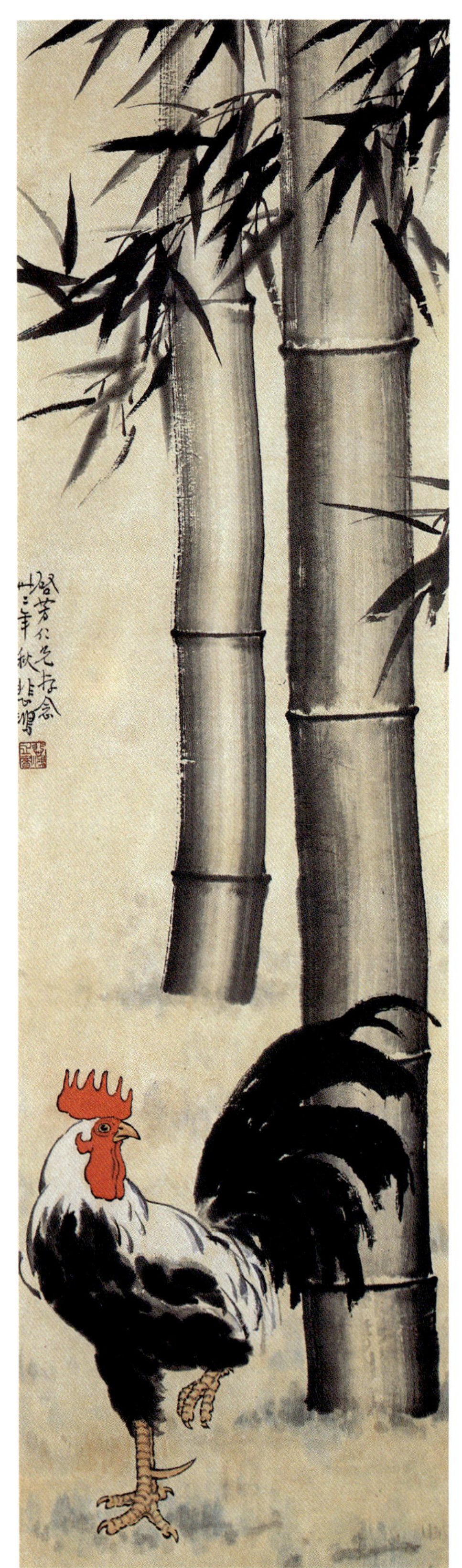

98

98   XU BEIHONG 徐悲鴻
1898–1953

Bamboo and Rooster

INK AND COLOUR ON PAPER
HANGING SCROLL, 118 × 34 CM
EA 1995.262
Inscribed: ＿ 芳仁兄存念 三十二年秋悲鴻
*A memento for Mr. Qi (?) Fang, autumn, 1943,
Beihong.*

Xu Beihong produced several rooster paintings in
the late 1930s and early 1940s; one example was
included in the large exhibiton of his work held in
Chengdu in 1943, the year in which the present
work was painted.

99   XU BEIHONG 徐悲鴻
1898–1953
HUANG ZHOU 黃冑
1925–

Herdboy and calligraphy
戊寅初春微雨放晴寫此遺興　悲鴻
牧牛圖　癸酉夏月於炎黃藝術館題悲鴻
大師　精品　今有幸見此眞跡佳
作亦非易也　黃冑

INK AND COLOUR AND INK ON PAPER
HORIZONTAL SCROLL, 55 × 50 AND 12.5 × 13.5 CM
EA 1995.263
Inscribed: 戊寅初春微雨放晴寫此遺興　悲鴻
*In early spring 1938 when the light rain was clearing
I drew this as a reminder　Beihong*

Herdboys were a subject favoured by Xu Beihong
for his paintings in Chinese style. The calligraphy is
by the much younger artist Huang Zhou and was
added in 1993 at Huang Zhou's own foundation
the Yanhuang Yishuguan; he places this amongst
the *jingpin* (finest work) of Xu Beihong.

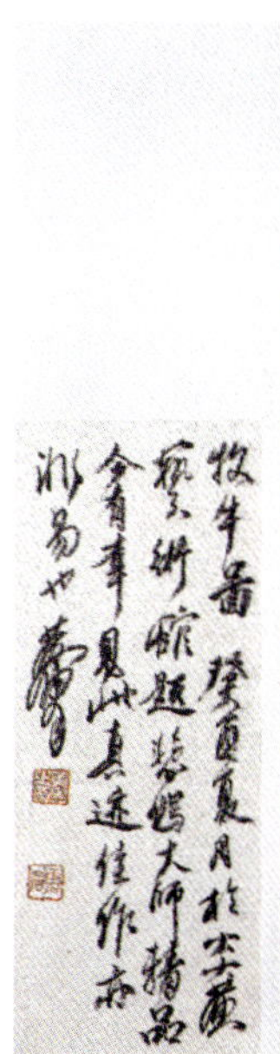
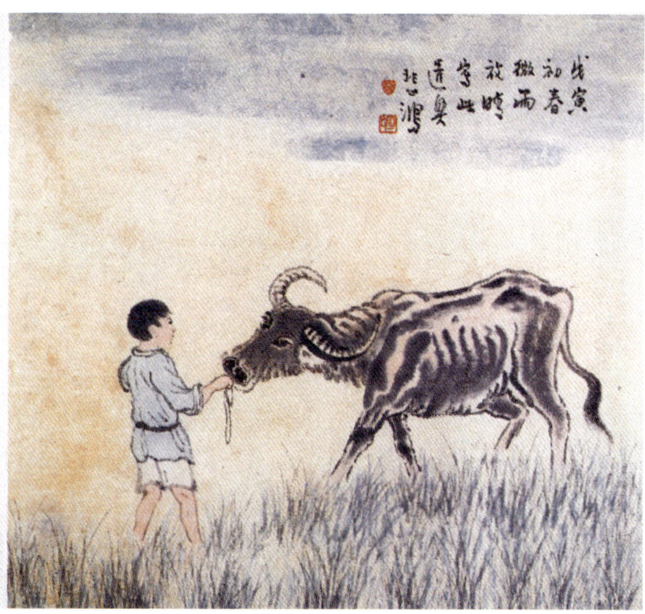

99

100 XU BEIHONG 徐悲鴻
1898–1953

Guilin landscape

INK ON PAPER, POSSIBLY A WOODBLOCK
REPRODUCTION

HANGING SCROLL, FRAMED, 49.5 × 74 CM

EA 1995.264

Inscribed: 漓江春雨 二十六年三月悲鴻
Spring rain on the Li River, Beihong March 1937

The Li river and the mountains of Guilin in the
southwestern province of Guangxi are amongst
China's most famous scenery. Xu Beihong visited
the area in the late 1930s and produced a landscape
closely comparable to the present work, but on a
much larger scale, and including in the inscription a
dedication to his future wife.

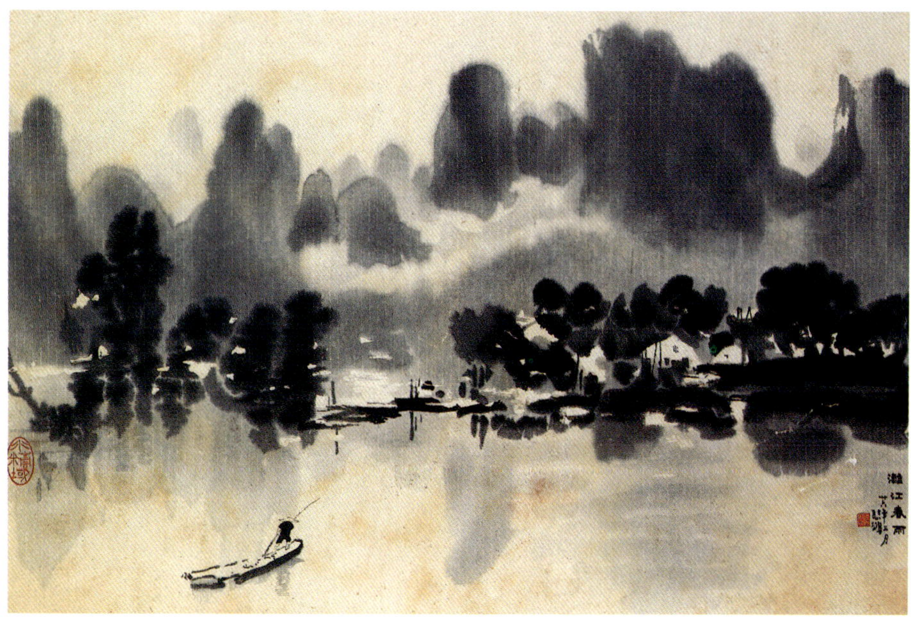

100

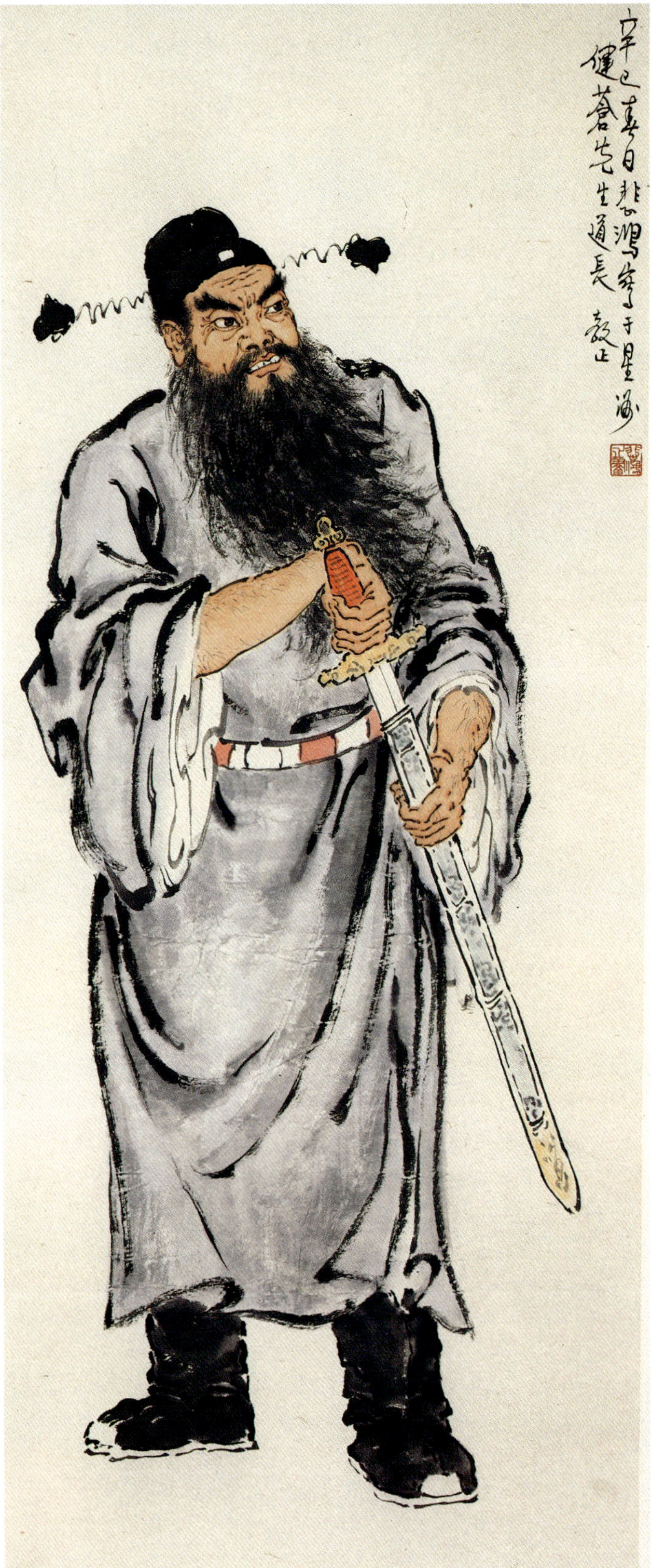

101

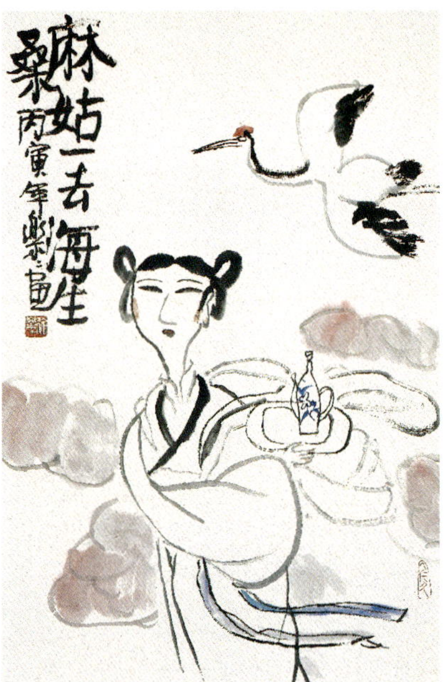

104

101 XU BEIHONG 徐悲鴻
1898–1953

Zhong Kui the Demon Queller

INK AND COLOUR ON PAPER

HANGING SCROLL, 104 × 44 CM

EA 1995.265

Inscribed: 辛巳春日悲鴻寫于星洲 健蒼先生道長敎正
*Drawn at Xingzhou in spring 1941 (by) Beihong
Presented to Mr. Jian Cang*

Xu Beihong's figures include oils and charcoal
drawings in western style, as well as didactic scenes
from Chinese legend. Single figures such as this
Zhong Kui are less common, yet Xu has retained in
this example the musculature and detail more
familiar in European than Chinese drawing.

102 XU GU 虛谷
1823–96

Squirrel

INK AND COLOUR ON PAPER

FAN PAINTING, FRAMED, L.53.5 CM

EA 1995.266

Inscribed: 寫於覺非盦 虛谷
Drawn at Juefeian, Xu Gu

Xu Gu came from a military family in Anhui
province and was associated with artistic circles in
Yangzhou, and later with the Shanghai School. His
paintings often combine precise, dry brushwork
with a looser style, as can be seen here in the
contrast between the execution of the squirrel and
the plants. Juefeian is Xu Gu's studio name.

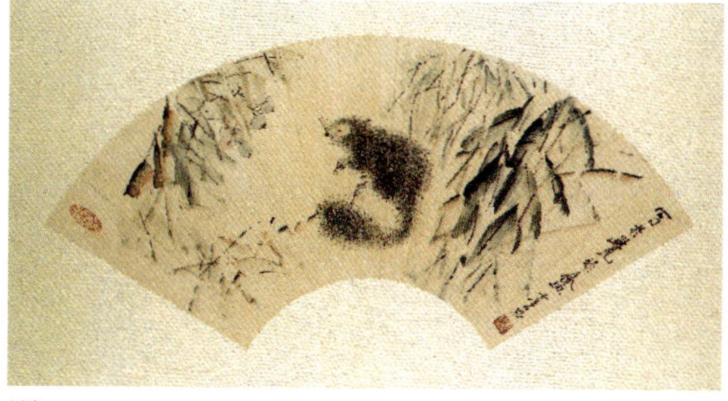

102

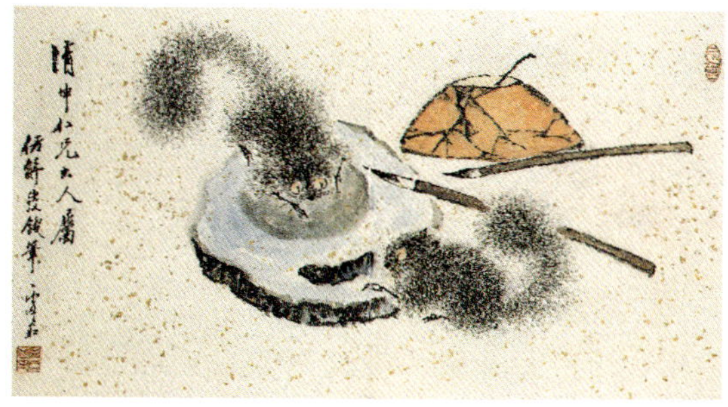

103

103 XU GU 虛谷
1823–96

Squirrels and inkstone

INK AND COLOUR ON GOLD-FLECKED PAPER

DOUBLE ALBUM-LEAF, FRAMED, 35 × 68.2 CM

EA 1995.267

Inscribed: 清申仁兄大人屬 仿解韜館筆 虛谷
*For Mr. Qing Shen   In the style of Hua Yan,
Xu Gu*

Xu Gu, a painter of plants and animals rather than
landscapes, is renowned for depicting popular
subjects in a disciplined manner, and his skill in
doing so is evident here. Squirrels and ornamental
goldfish are the subjects with which he is most
closely associated. Hua Yan (1682–1756) was one of
the painters known as the Eight Eccentrics of
Yangzhou, from whom the Shanghai School artists
drew inspiration. Yangzhou is also Xu Gu's native
town.

104 XU LELE 徐樂樂
1955–

Figure with bird

INK AND COLOUR ON PAPER

HANGING SCROLL, FRAMED, 68 × 45.2 CM

EA 1995.268

Inscribed: 麻姑一去海生桑 丙寅年樂樂畫
*After Magu has gone, the sea becomes land
1986, painted (by) Lele*

Magu is a female immortal in Chinese mythology
and is depicted here as a Tang figure, though she is
painted in a sweeping calligraphic style rather than
in the fine conventions of Tang figure painting. Xu
Lele studied at Nanjing Academy of Painting and
her style derives from the Shanghai School painters
Ren Xiong (1820–57) and Ren Yi (1840–95).

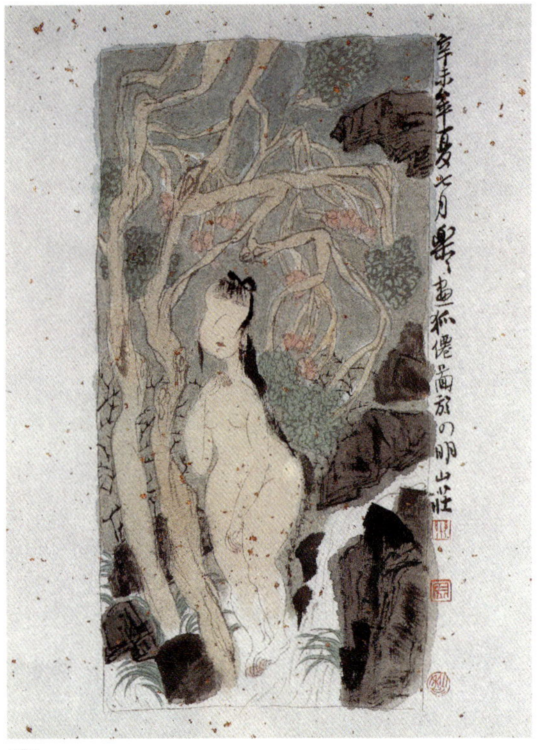

105a

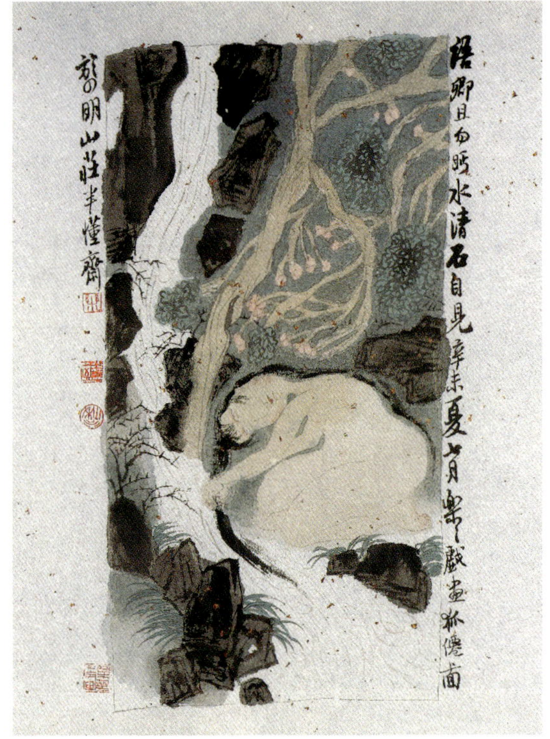

105b

105A XU LELE　徐樂樂
1955–

The Fox Fairy

INK AND COLOUR ON GOLD-FLECKED BLUE
PAPER

VERTICAL PAINTING IN WESTERN MOUNT,
FRAMED, 43 × 32 CM

EA 1995.269

Inscribed:
辛未年夏七月樂樂畫狐仙圖於四明山莊
*Summer 1991, Lele painted the Fox Fairy at Siming
Villa*

Xu Lele is a figure painter who takes her subjects
from popular literature. These two paintings depict
the Fox Fairy, subject of a Tang short story about a
beautiful young seductress who is really a fox fairy
in disguise, and having found a faithful lover is
eventually torn apart by hounds.

105B XU LELE　徐樂樂
1955–

The Fox Fairy

INK AND COLOUR ON GOLD-FLECKED BLUE
PAPER

VERTICAL PAINTING IN WESTERN MOUNT,
FRAMED, 43.5 × 32 CM

EA 1995.270

Inscribed:
語卿且勿晒水清石自見　辛未夏七月樂樂戲畫狐
仙圖於四明山莊　半懂齋

10-character inscription followed by
*Summer 1991, Lele painted the Fox Fairy at
Bandong Studio, Siming Villa*

This painting and its pair are unusual in that they
have been framed in pencil, and the calligraphy and
seals lie outside the composition. Plain or coloured
gold-flecked papers have been used for many
centuries.

106 YA MING　亞明

1924–

River landscape

INK AND COLOUR ON PAPER

HANGING SCROLL, FRAMED, 67 × 44.6 CM

EA 1995.271

Inscribed: 暮秋　乙丑年孟夏寫於金陵亞明
Late autumn, painted (by) Ya Ming at Jinling
(Nanjing) in the first month of summer, 1985

Ya Ming was a pupil of Fu Baoshi and the style here
is reminiscent of Fu's views of cities in eastern
Europe, particularly in the dry ink brushwork on
the distant trees.

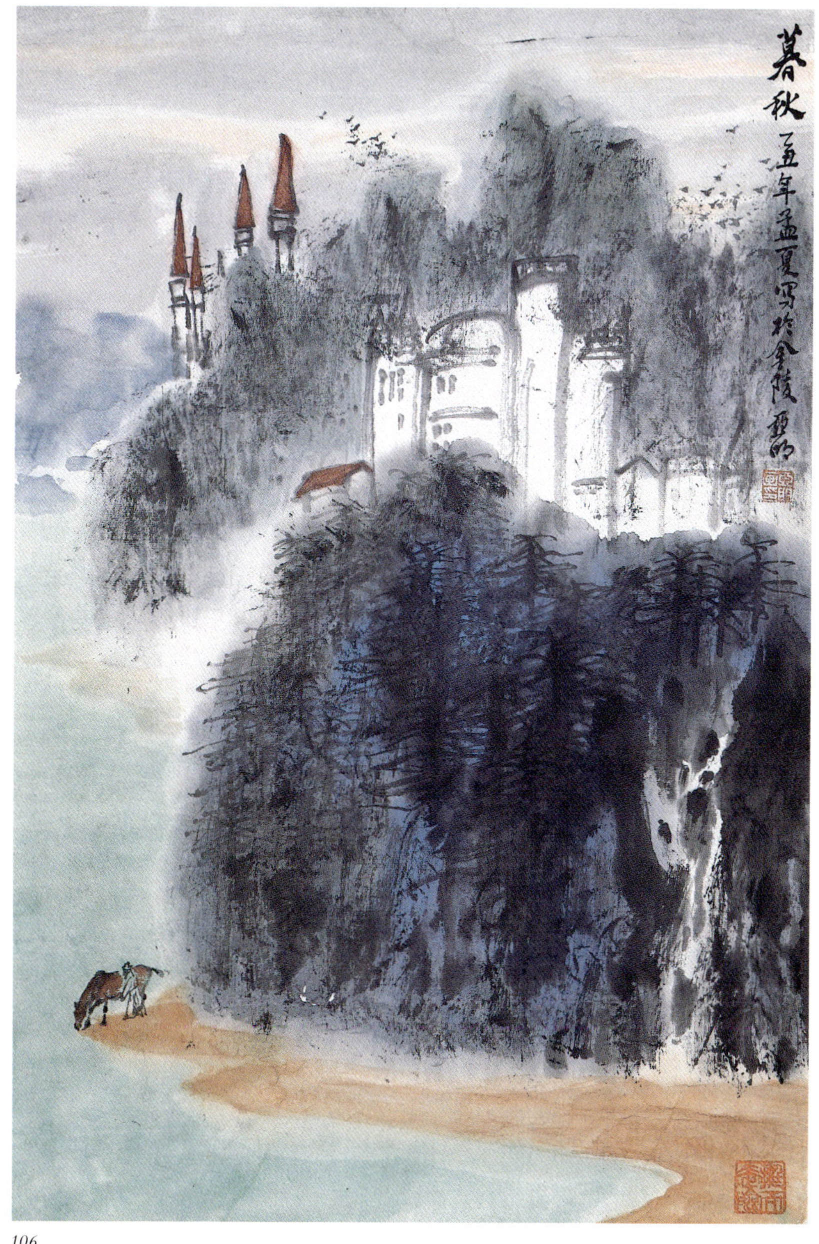

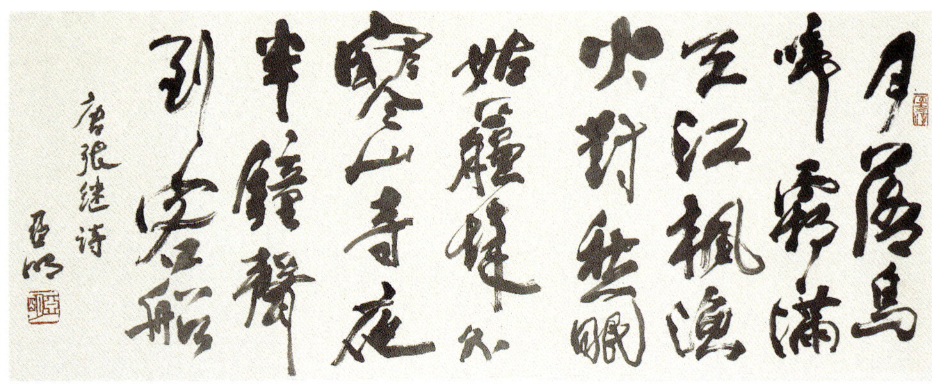

107

107 YA MING 亞明
1924–

Calligraphy　月落烏啼霜滿天
江楓漁火對愁眠　姑蘇城外
寒山寺　夜半鍾聲到客船

INK ON PAPER
HORIZONTAL SCROLL, MOUNTED ON SILK
33.4 × 89 CM
EA 1995.299
Inscribed: 唐張繼詩 亞明
Poem by Zhang Ji of the Tang Ya Ming

The calligraphy comprises a famous Tang dynasty
poem by Zhang Ji, but is executed in the style of
the great calligraphers of the Song (960–1279)
dynasty.

108 YANG SHANSHEN 楊善深
1913–

Landscape

INK AND COLOUR ON PAPER
HANGING SCROLL, 68 × 34 CM
EA 1995.272
Inscribed: 蒼茫野色几沙灘　漳水東流倚堞看
煙火滿城天向夕 ＿ 鴉飛過不知寒
28-character poem
Signed:　善深　*Shanshen* (twice)

Yang Shanshen, also known as Yang Shen-sum,
followed Gao Jianfu and is known as one of the
second generation of Lingnan School painters. His
technique for painting trees and rocks is to use the
split tip of a worn-out soft goat's hair brush, thus
leaving blank areas within inkstrokes. The poem in
the inscription is on the theme of crows, which can
be seen here on the rock and in the upper branches
of the tree.

109 YANG ZHENGXIN 楊正新
1942–

Variation in Landscape 2

INK AND COLOUR ON PAPER
SQUARE PAINTING IN WESTERN MOUNT,
FRAMED, 61.3 × 60.4 CM
EA 1995.273
Signed:　楊正新　　*Yang Zhengxin*

Yang Zhengxin, of Shanghai Art Academy, is a
traditionally-trained painter who experiments with
new structures in landscape painting. Much of his
work is semi-abstract.

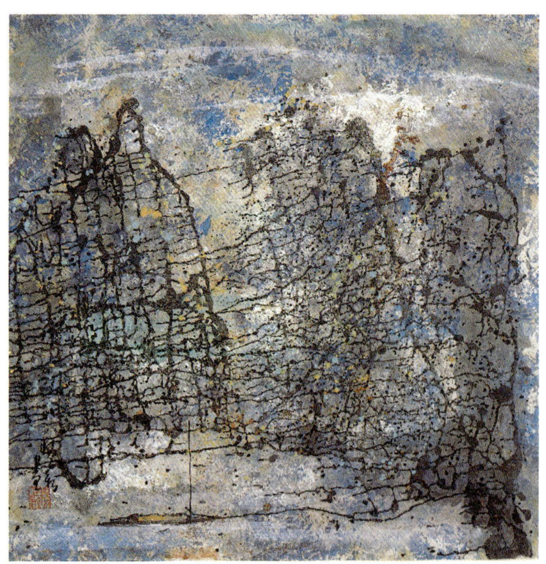

109

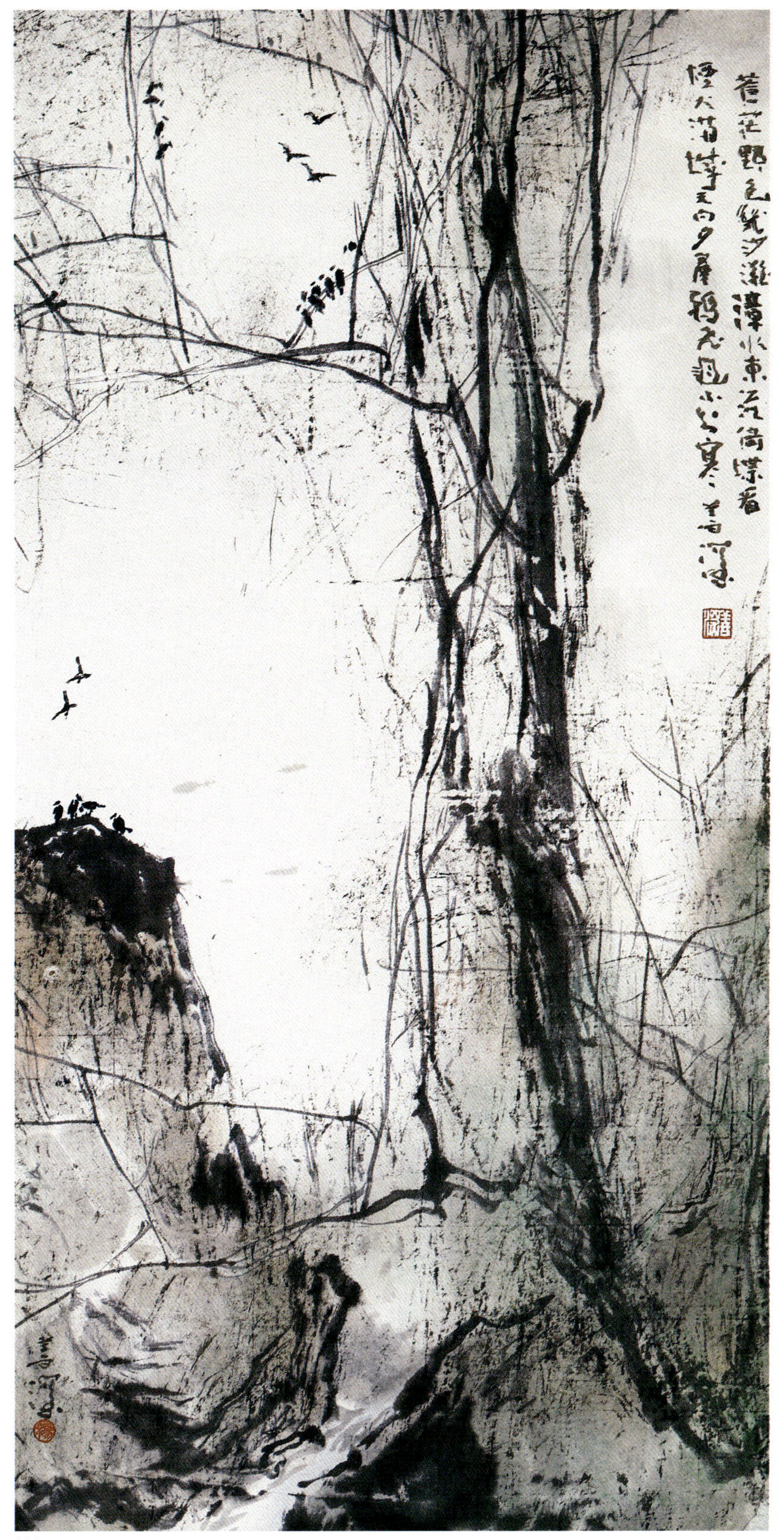

舊花野色覺少邐潭水東流尚凜冽
煙火滿博文之夕屢鴉飛過小於寒 中道河清

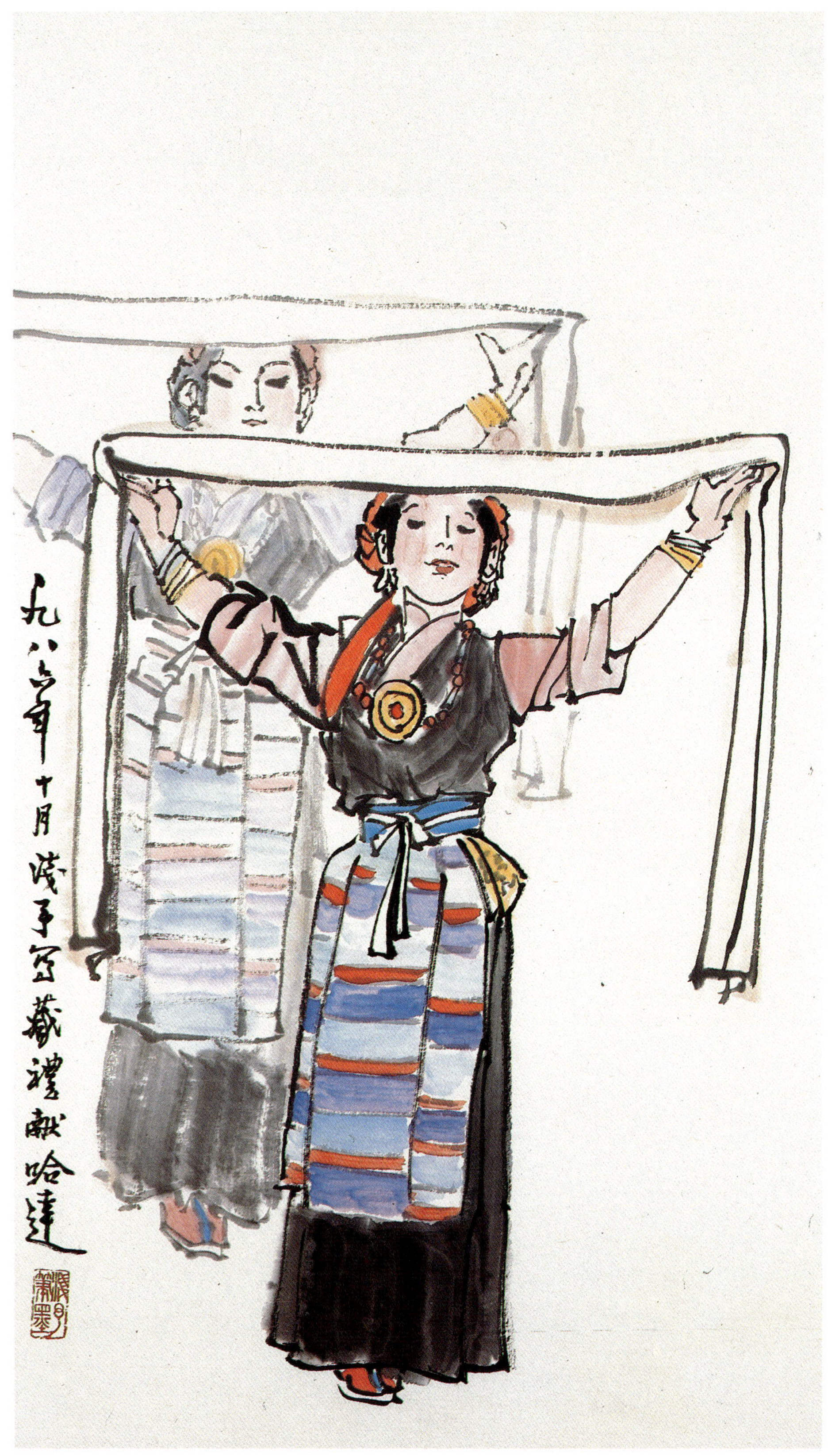

110

110 YE QIANYU 葉淺予
1907–

Figure

INK AND COLOUR ON PAPER

HANGING SCROLL, FRAMED, 91 × 52.6 CM

EA 1995.274

Inscribed: 一九八六年十月淺予寫藏禮獻哈達
1986, October, Qianyu painted the Tibetan hada

Ye Qianyu trained as an illustrator of advertisements, books and comics. He specialises in dancing figures and in particular those of China's ethnic minorities. This painting depicts the customary Tibetan presentation of hada (lengths of white silk) as a greeting to guests.

111 YU FEI'AN 于非闇
1889–1959

Bird on a flowering branch

INK AND COLOUR ON PAPER

FAN PAINTING, FRAMED, L. 48.6 CM

EA 1995.275

Inscribed: 壬午三月二十七日制此圖時正狂風大作也非闇
On 27 April 1942 a gale blew as (I) created this picture Fei'an

Yu Fei'an was a traditional painter active in Peking in the early twentieth century. The flat red and green colour within hard black outlines is typical of his flower painting style, which derives ultimately from Song (960-1279) court painting. Yu Fei'an, somewhat unusually for a Chinese painter, was particularly interested in colour and is the author of a book on the subject.

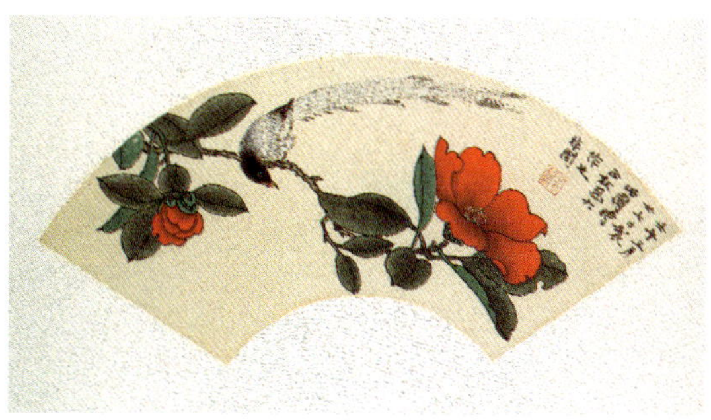

111

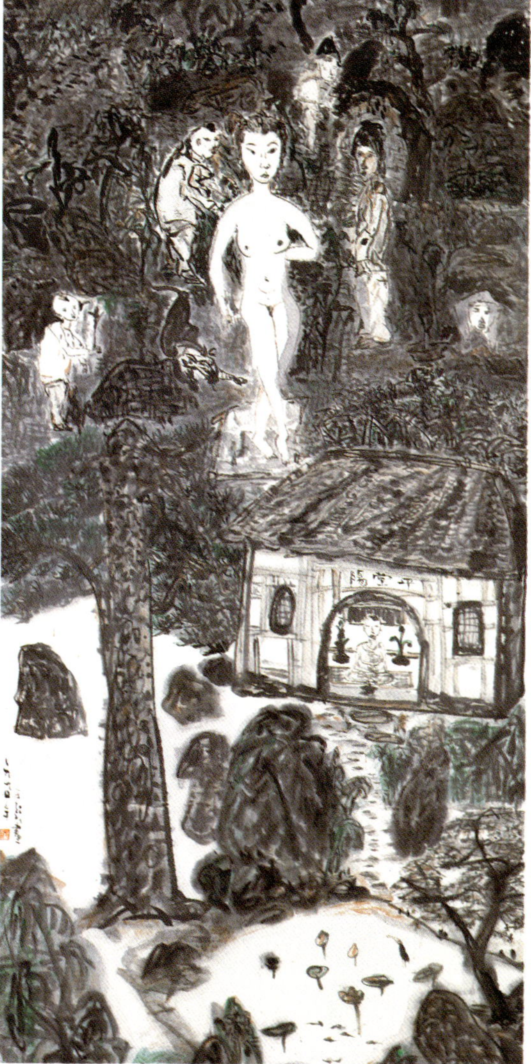

112

112 YU PENG 于彭
1955–

Little Yu at Zen

INK AND COLOUR ON PAPER

HANGING SCROLL, FRAMED, 135 × 69 CM

EA 1995.298

Inscribed: 于彭畫 一九九〇 年
Yu Peng, 1990

Yu Peng from Taiwan uses foreign pigments and rough brushwork to produce landscapes with a traditional flavour. The artist's family are frequently incorporated in the composition, which in this case may be loosely compared to Buddhist paradise paintings of the ninth century.

113 ZHANG DAQIAN 張大千
1899–1983

Dunhuang goddess

INK AND COLOUR ON SILK

HANGING SCROLL, FRAMED, 101.6 × 39.4 CM

EA 1995.276

Inscribed:
34-character inscription ending
仿莫高窟唐人 ＿＿ 供養天女 大千居士
*Tang dynasty attendant goddess, after the Mogao caves,
Daqian*

In 1942 Zhang Daqian travelled to Dunhuang to
visit the famous Mogao Buddhist cave temples, and
in the following two years produced many copies of
the Tang (618–906) dynasty murals he saw there.
The linear style and absence of background are
features of Tang figure painting.

114 ZHANG DAQIAN 張大千
1899–1983

Landscape

INK AND LIGHT COLOUR ON PAPER

FAN PAINTING, FRAMED, L. 53 CM

EA 1995.277

Inscribed: 六十七年戊午秋日寫此蕭原仁兄方家法教
八十叟爰
*1967 autumn painted for Xiao Yuan 80-year-old
man, Yuan*

The artist and forger Zhang Daqian was one of the
most successful painters of the twentieth century,
renowned for his skill and his versatility. He left
China in the 1940s and lived in many diffeerent
countries, including Brazil. This landscape
composition fully exploits the fan format, while the
extensive ink wash may be compared with his work
on a much larger scale. Yuan was Zhang Daqian's
alternative name.

115 ZHANG DAQIAN 張大千
1899–1983

Lotus

INK AND COLOUR ON PAPER

HORIZONTAL SCROLL, FRAMED, 59.4 × 83.5 CM

EA 1995.278

Inscribed:
40-character inscription ending
六十九年秋寫此頌蘭夫人雅教 八十二叟爰 摩耶精舍
*Drawn in autumn for Mme. Song Lan the sixty-ninth
year (by) eighty-two-year-old Yuan staying at Moye
jingshe*

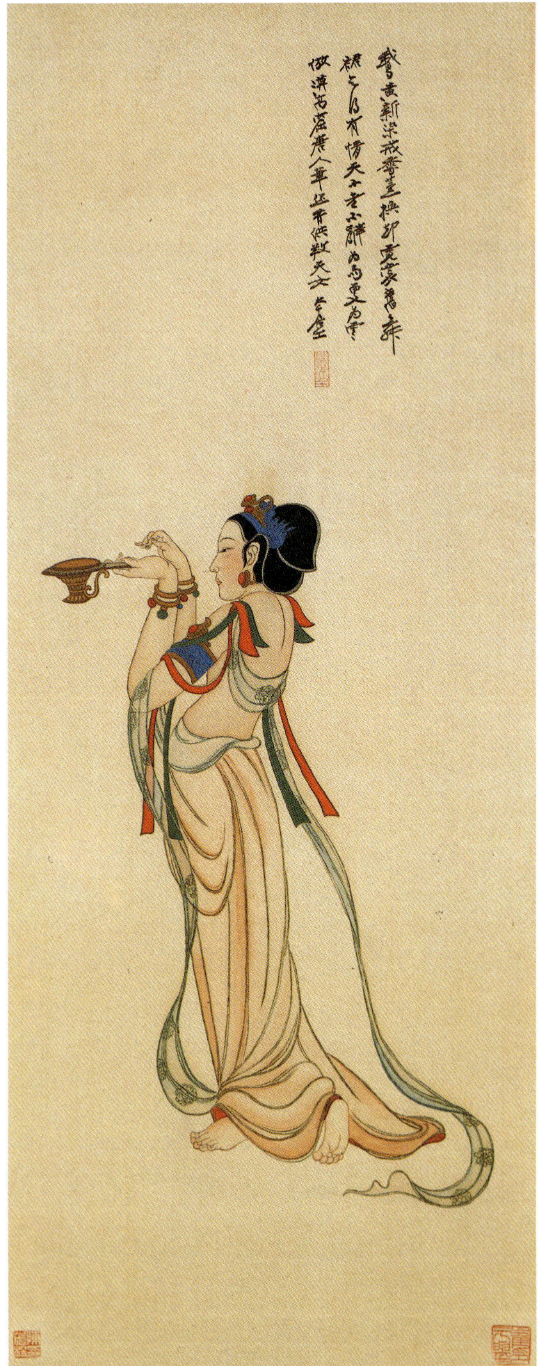

113

Zhang Daqian cultivated elaborate gardens in all the
residences he occupied in his peripatetic life, and
exhorted other artists, if they wished to paint
flowers, to surround themselves with plants. His
lotus paintings in the present style, combining
careful brushwork with colour and ink washes, are a
well known and influential type.

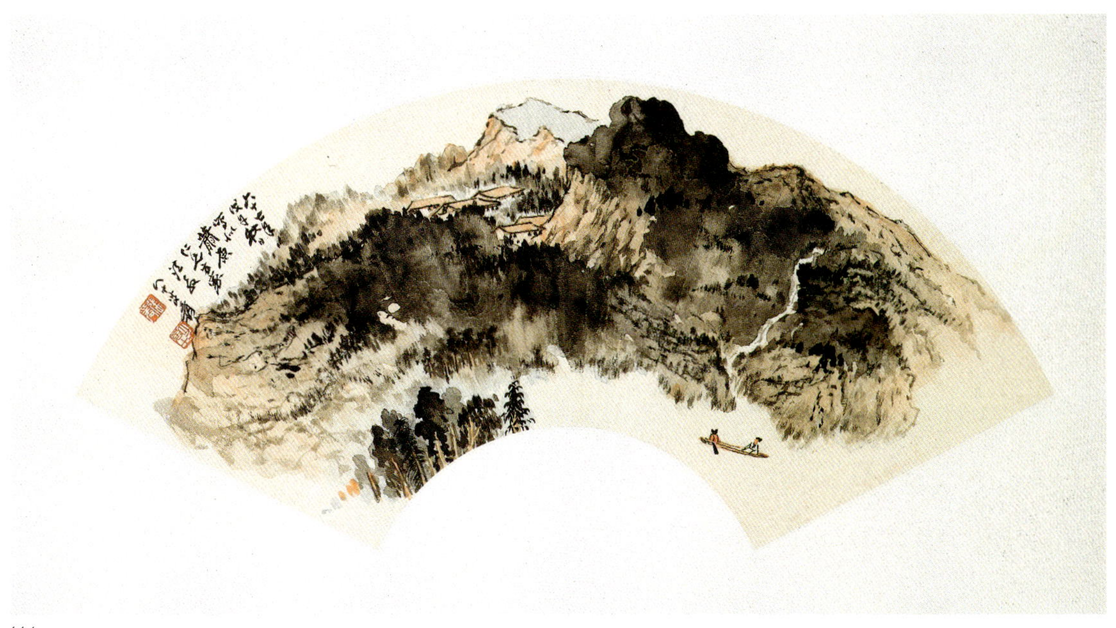

114

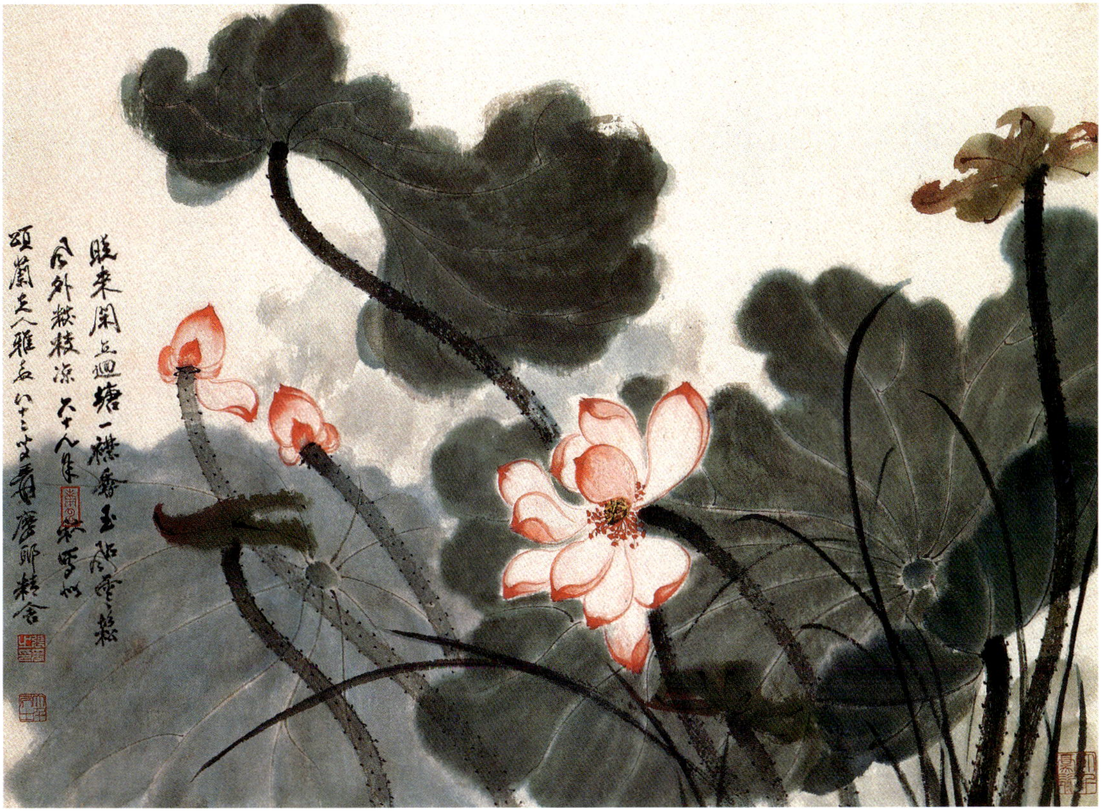

115

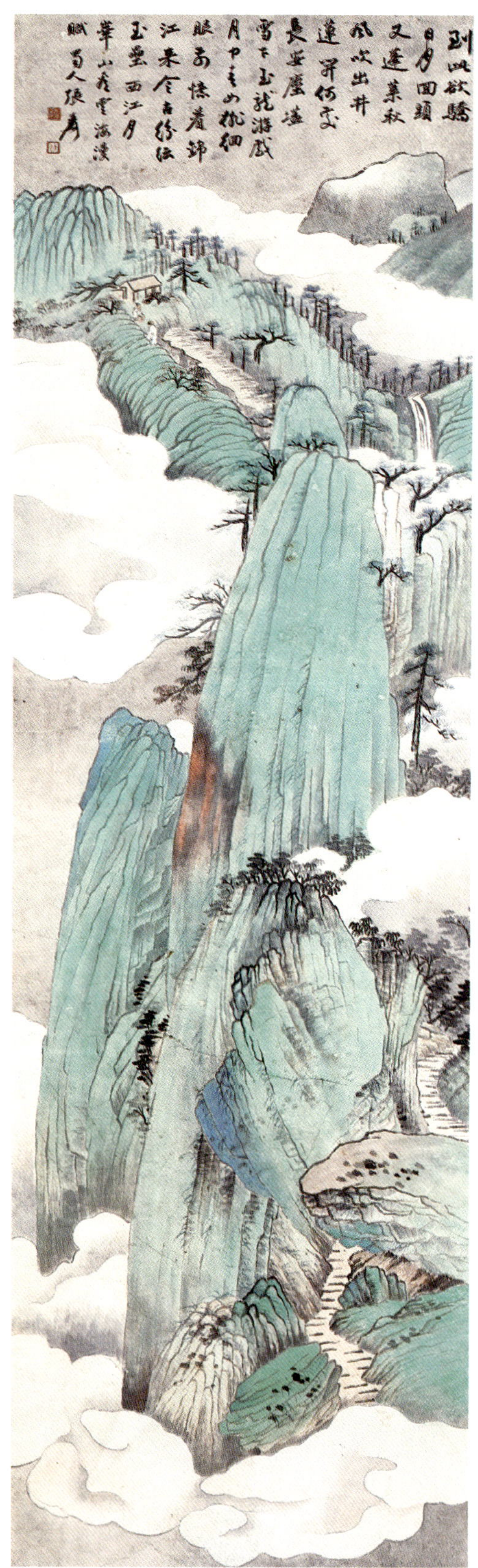

116

116 ZHANG DAQIAN 張大千
1899–1983

Landscape in archaic style

INK AND COLOUR ON PAPER
HANGING SCROLL, FRAMED, 136 × 41.2 CM
EA 1995.279
Inscribed:
63-character inscription ending 蜀人張爰
Zhang Yuan of Sichuan

The bright green colour and the hard outlines of
the mountains and clouds evoke Tang (618-906)
dynasty landscape style. The perspective, in which
there is no proper receding ground but in which
the eye is led up the zig-zagging composition to the
relatively large figures in the background, is also
inspired by the Tang murals at Dunhuang.

117 ZHANG DAQIAN 張大千
1899–1983

and PU RU 溥儒
1896–1963

Scholar by a tree

INK AND COLOUR ON PAPER
HANGING SCROLL, 105 × 38 CM
EA 1995.280
Inscribed: 甲戌嘉平月大千居士爰 , *February 1934,*
Daqian the lay Buddhist Yuan and 心畬補松 ,
Xinyu (painted the) pine

In the 1920s Pu Ru and Zhang Daqian were the
acknowledged masters of traditional painting in
north and south China respectively. When Zhang
moved to Peking the two became friends,
collaborating on several paintings and living for some
years as neighbours in the former imperial summer
palace. Both championed traditional painting yet the
contrast between Pu's careful style and Zhang's free
brushwork is evident in this scroll.

118 ZHANG DAQIAN 張大千
1899–1983

Scholar beneath trees

INK AND COLOUR ON PAPER
HANGING SCROLL, FRAMED, 125.3 × 46 CM
EA 1995.281
Inscribed: 蜀人大千居士張爰
Daqian of Sichuan the lay Buddhist Zhang Yuan

The loose brushwork and green tree-trunks lend
modernity to this traditional subject of a solitary
scholar amongst trees. It is possibly a self-portrait.

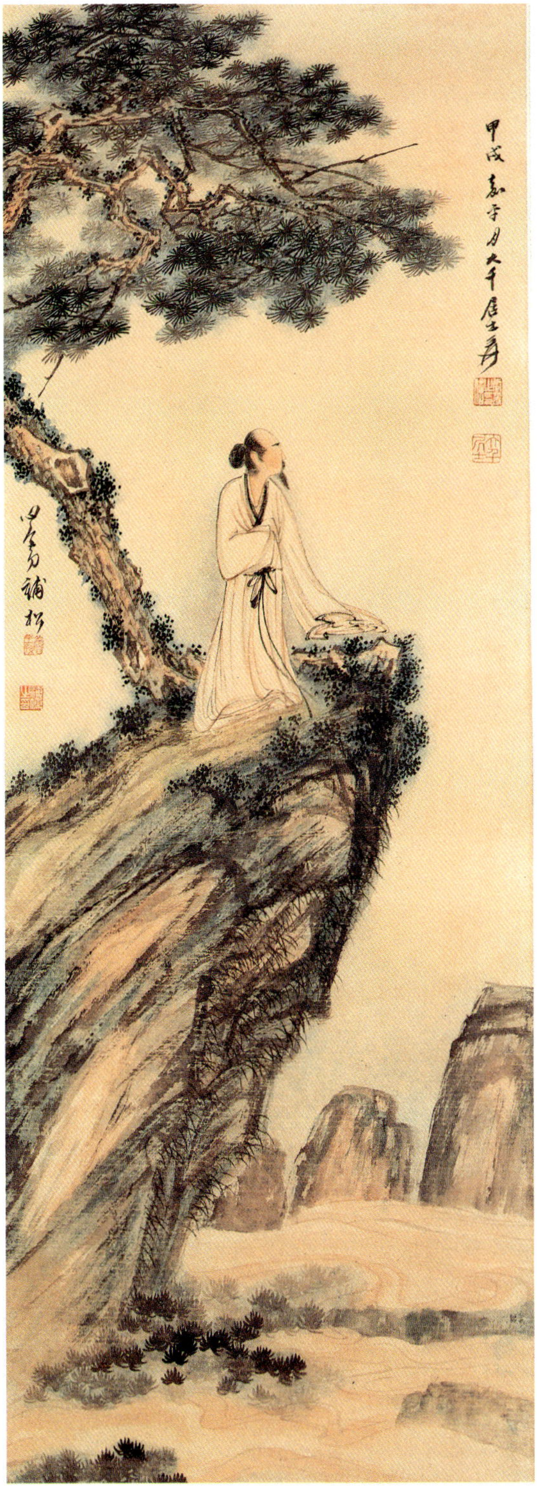

117

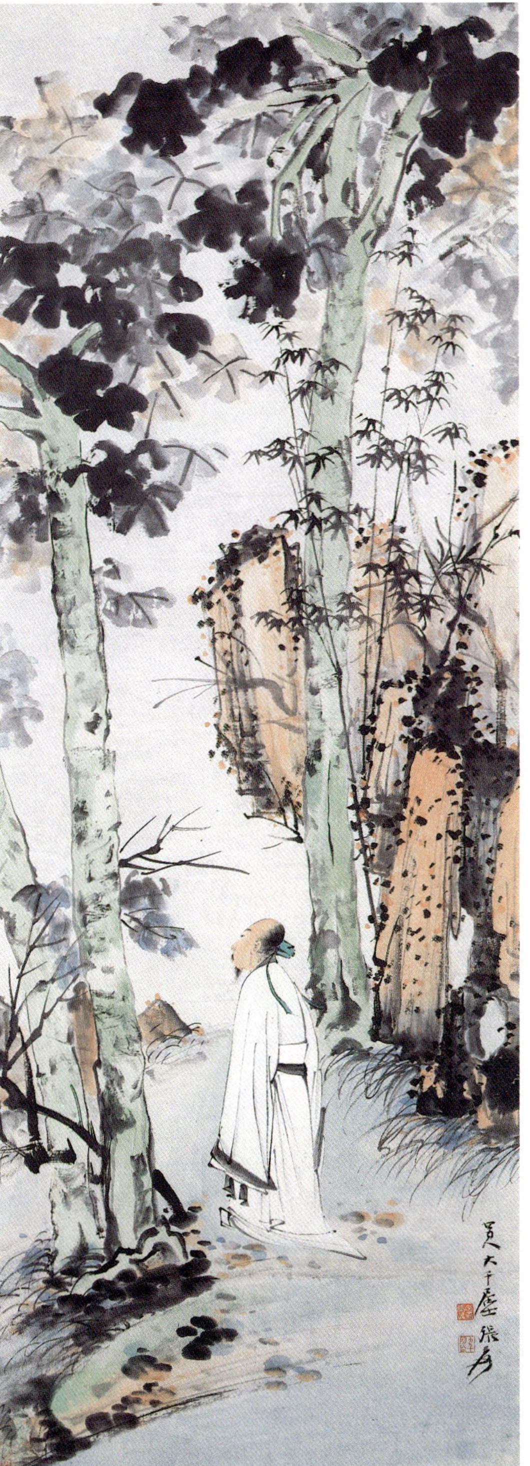

118

119 ZHAO SHAO'ANG 趙少昂
1905–

Calligraphy

INK ON PAPER

PAIR OF HANGING SCROLLS, FRAMED, EACH
134 × 30 CM

EA 1995.282 a,b

Inscribed: 尹民醫師雅屬　已未春二月趙少昂書
*For Dr. Yi Min, February 1979, written (by) Zhao
Shao'ang*

Zhao Shao'ang is one of the second generation of
Lingnan School artists. This couplet of two five-
character lines is executed in his distinctive angular
style.

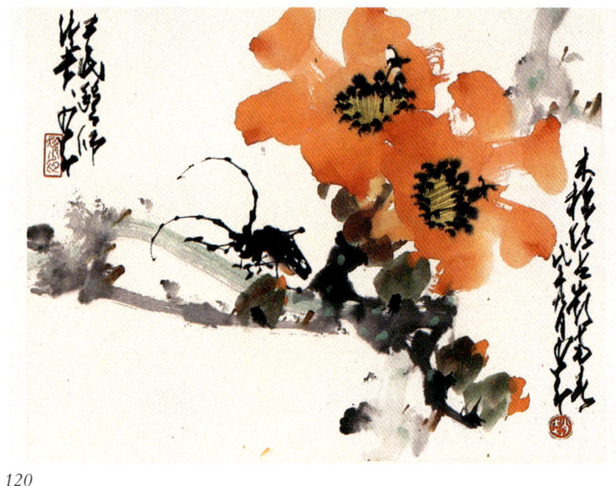

120

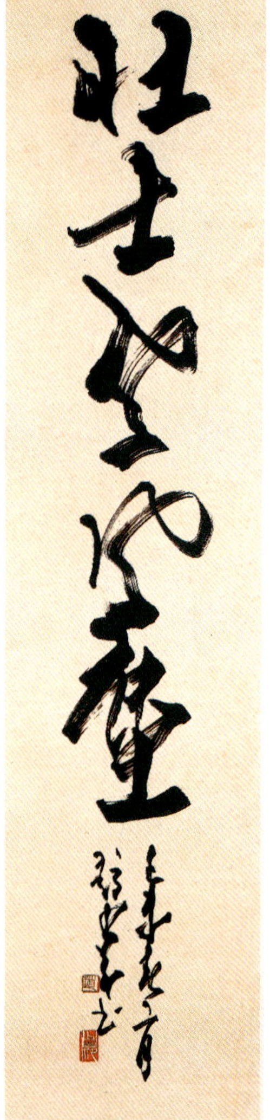

119

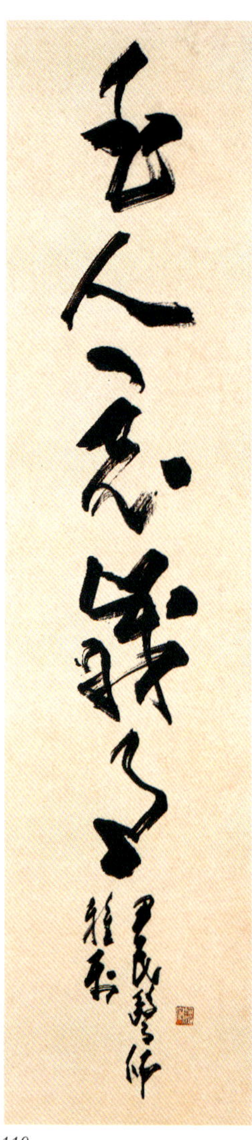

119

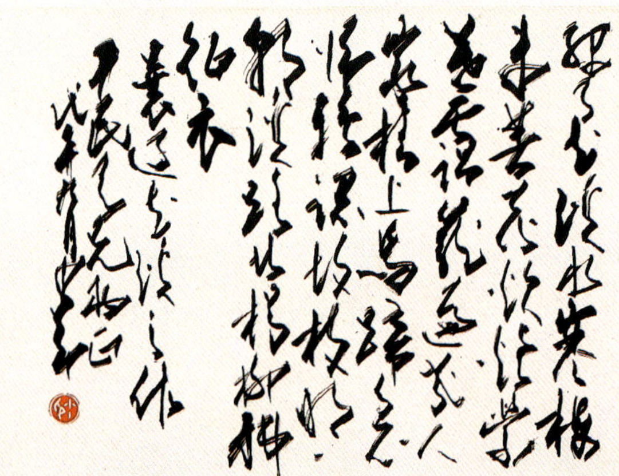

120b

120 ZHAO SHAO'ANG 趙少昂
1905–

Flower and calligraphy

INK AND COLOUR AND INK ON PAPER

TWO ALBUM LEAVES, MOUNTED TOGETHER
AND FRAMED, EACH 30.1 × 37.6 CM

EA 1995.283 a,b

Inscribed: 木棉 ＿ 占嶺南春 戊午九月少昂
尹民醫師清賞少昂
(a): *Painted for Dr. Yi Min, the kapok flower
flourishes in spring in Lingnan, 1978 Shao'ang*

b): poem composed by the artist, signed and
dated 1978

Zhao Shao'ang produced many flower paintings in
this vivid style, and often mixed his seal paste to
match the colours of the blooms. The strong light
vermilion of the seal on this album leaf is in
harmony with the orange kapok flower, a common
plant in the Lingnan area of south China.

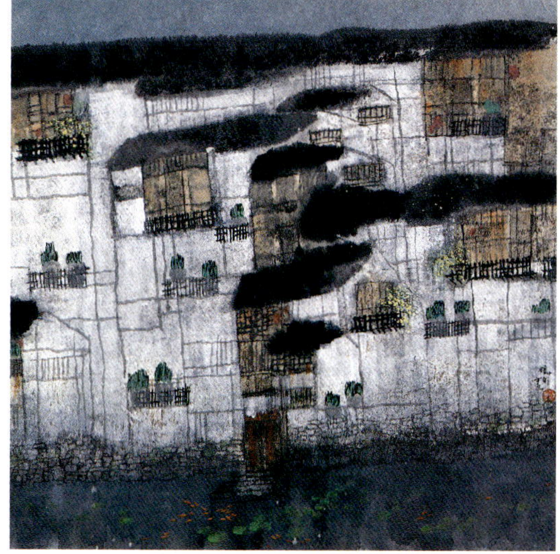

121 ZHAO ZHUNWANG 趙准旺
1944–

Houses

INK AND COLOUR ON PAPER

SQUARE PAINTING, IN WESTERN MOUNT,
FRAMED, 68 × 65 CM

EA 1995.284

Signed: 准旺畫

Painted (by) Zhunwang

Zhao Zhunwang is a Beijing artist known for
paintings of towns or villages combining square
blocks of ink or colour wash with colour dots, or
dian. He is from Jiangsu, and the canal depicted
here is typical both of the region and of his
compositions.

122 ZHENG WUCHANG 鄭午昌
1894–1952

Landscape

INK AND COLOUR ON PAPER

HANGING SCROLL, FRAMED, 62 × 169 CM

EA 1995.285

Inscribed: 萬壑千峰明積玉小橋曲港靜尋詩 狀雪不粉
亦宋人法也 丁亥鄭午昌寫

14-character couplet followed by
*Painting snow without using white colour is the Song
method, 1947, written (by) Zheng Wuchang*

Zheng Wuchang was one of the leading art
historians of the early twentieth century. His
paintings are conservative and typically name in
their inscriptions the paintings and art historical
theories to which they relate.

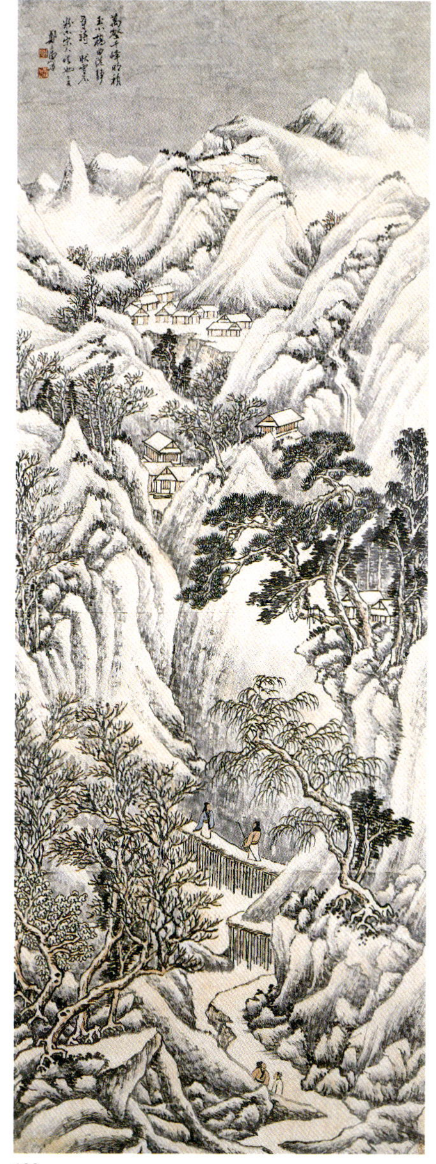

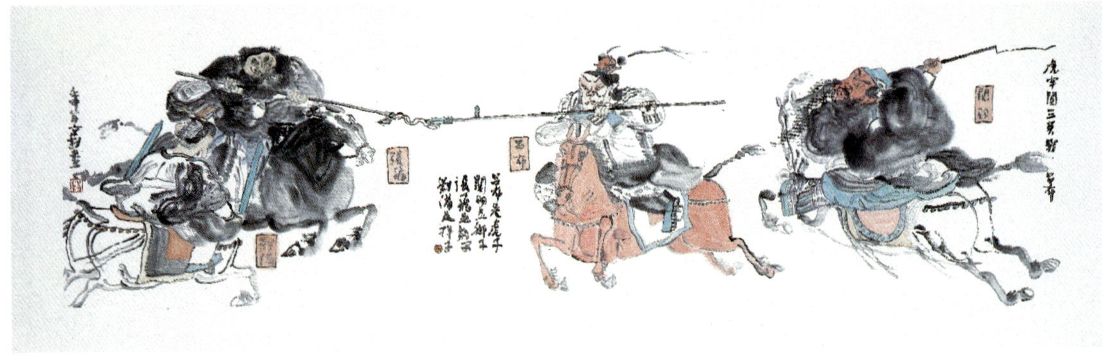

123

123 ZHOU JINGXIN 周京新
1959–

Liu Bei and others

INK AND COLOUR ON PAPER
HORIZONTAL SCROLL, FRAMED, 34 × 136.5 CM
EA 1995.286
Inscribed: 虎牢關三英雄戰呂布　壬申年京新畫
*The three heroes fighting Lu Bu at Hulaoguan
1992, painted (by) Jingxin*

Zhou Jingxin is well-known for his paintings of
figures from vernacular fiction. Liu Bei, Zhang Jue
and Guan Yu are the heroes of the Ming novel
Sanguo yanyi "Three Kingdoms", by Luo
Guanzhong. Such heroes have a long history of
representation in woodblock illustrations and on
porcelain, where they appear similarly labelled.

124 ZHOU JINGXIN 周京新
1959–

*Scenes from the Romance of the Three
Kingdoms*

INK AND COLOUR ON PAPER
ALBUM OF TEN LEAVES, EACH 34.5 × 34.5 CM
EA 1995.294 a–j
Each leaf inscribed and signed: 京新畫
Painted (by) Jingxin

The scene illustrated here is the opening leaf of the
album. Dated 1992 and entitled *The Oath in the
Peach Garden* it depicts the episode in which the
three heroes of the novel swear allegiance to one
another. The robust style of the painting is suited to
the swashbuckling, popular nature of the novel.

125 ZHU QIZHAN 朱屺瞻
1892–1996

Landscape

INK AND COLOUR ON PAPER
HANGING SCROLL, FRAMED, 96.4 × 61.2 CM
EA 1995.287
Signed 屺瞻 *Qizhan*

Zhu Qizhan lived and worked in Shanghai and is
one of the major artists of the twentieth century.
He studied in Japan and from his twenties until his
fifties painted in oils as well as the Chinese medium.
The simplicity and colour of this landscape are
typical of the distinctive style he developed.

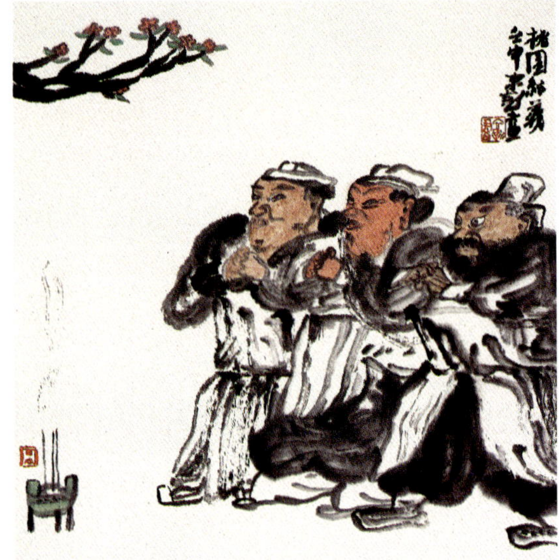

124

90

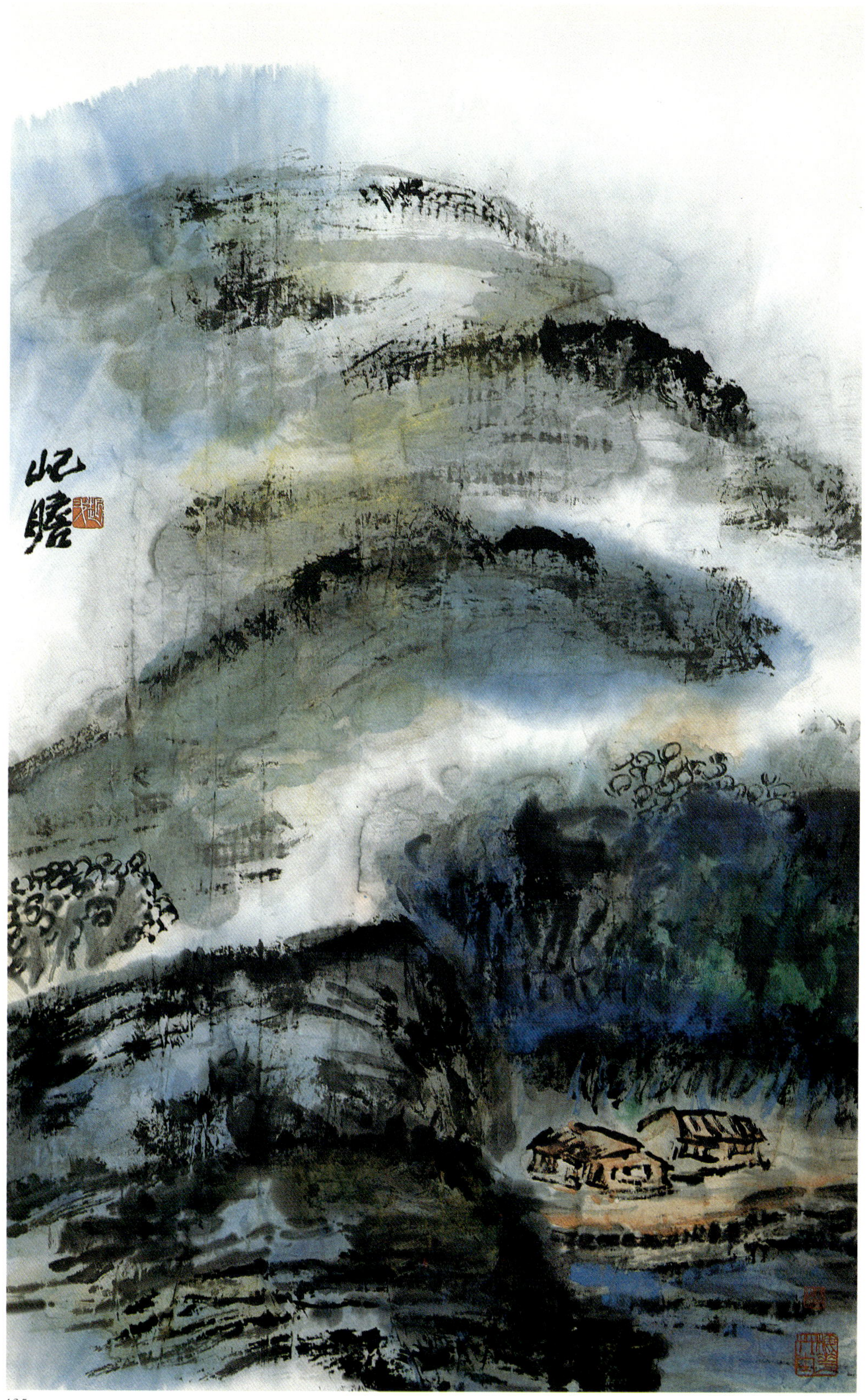

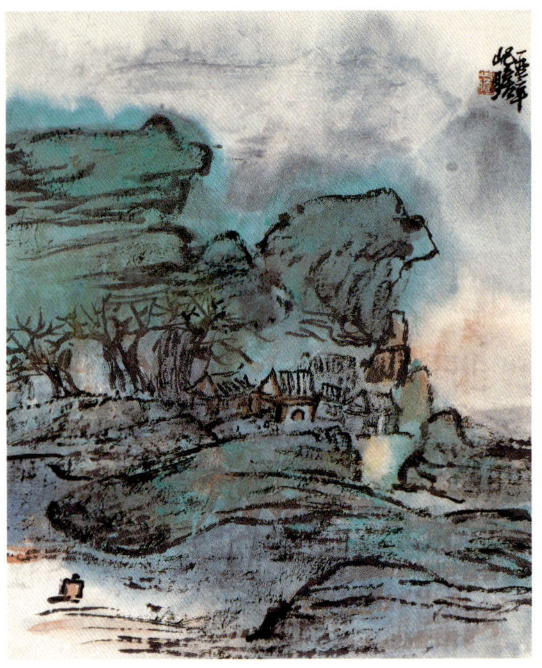

126

127 ZHU QIZHAN 朱屺瞻
1892–1996

River village

INK AND COLOUR ON PAPER
HANGING SCROLL, FRAMED, 50.5 × 69.2 CM
EA 1995.289
Inscribed: 漁村　瞻潑墨甲子大暑
Qizhan splashing ink in high summer, 1984

The term *pomo* in the inscription means "splashed ink" and refers to an 8th century technique in which quantities of ink were applied directly to silk or paper and only brushed after forming pools. It is the opposite of using a calligraphic line, and combined here with slight colour gives an undoubtedly modern look to a traditional composition.

126 ZHU QIZHAN 朱屺瞻
1892–1996

Landscape

INK AND COLOUR ON PAPER
HANGING SCROLL, FRAMED, 42 × 35.8 CM
EA 1995.288
Inscribed: 一九七二年　屺瞻
1972, Qizhan

Zhu Qizhan's three stated aims in painting are independence, force (or strength) and succinctness. This sketchy yet vivid landscape in his own style appears to embody these ideals.

128 ZHU WEI 朱偉
1966–

Figures

INK AND COLOUR ON PAPER
SQUARE PAINTING, MOUNTED IN SILK,
FRAMED, 66.7 × 66.7 CM
EA 1995.291
Inscribed: 愛人 我要和你去戰斗. 只要我們還有一口氣,
我們就不能停止戰斗. 只要我們還有一口氣,
就必須把手中的武器牢牢抓緊.

My love, I want to go forward into battle with you; as long as there is breath left in us we will never retreat, as long as there is breath left in us we will hold our weapons firm

Zhu Wei belongs to the post-1989 generation of painters associated with the Political Pop and Cynical Realism movements. He was formerly in the People's Liberation Army and trained at the PLA Art Academy. Seals have been incorporated into the composition of this painting and the words inscribed on it are probably from a Cantonese pop song.

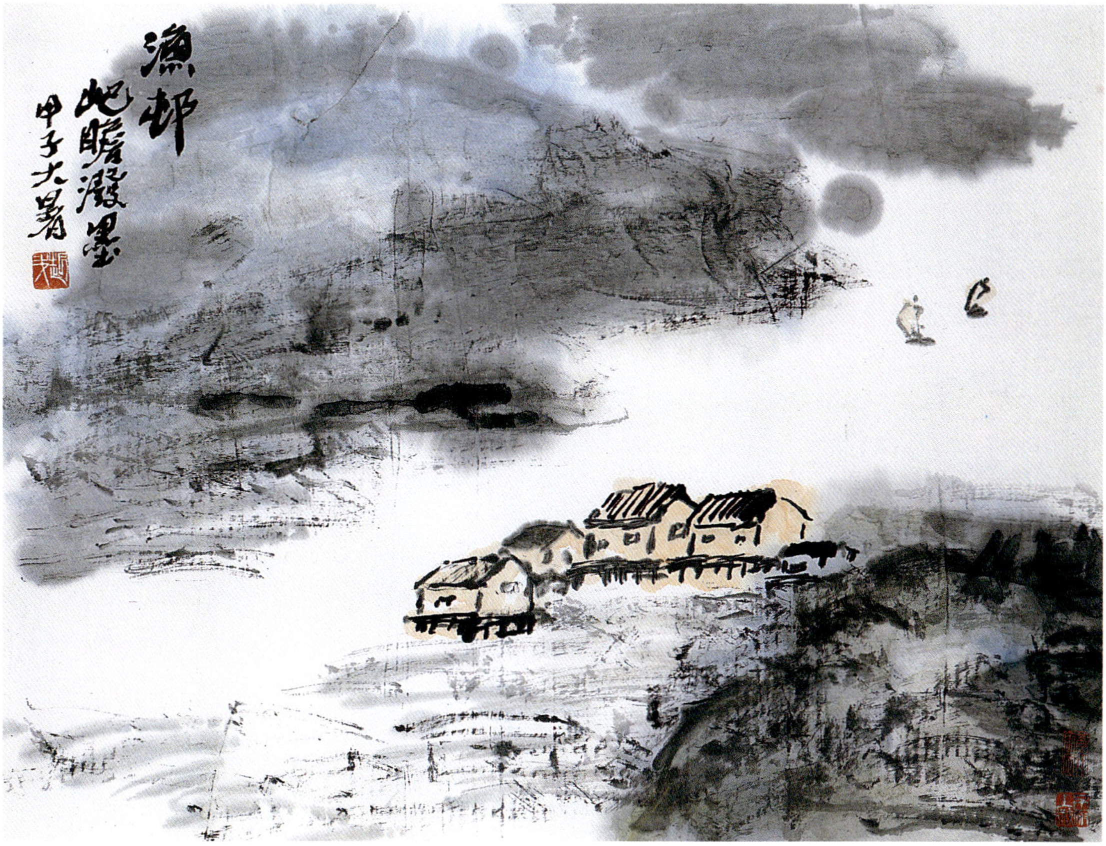

127

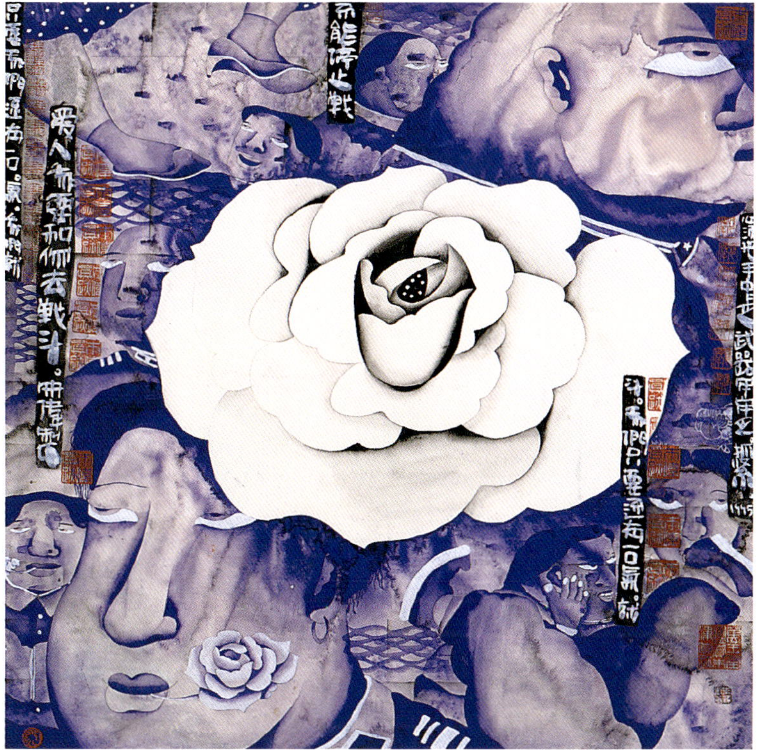

128

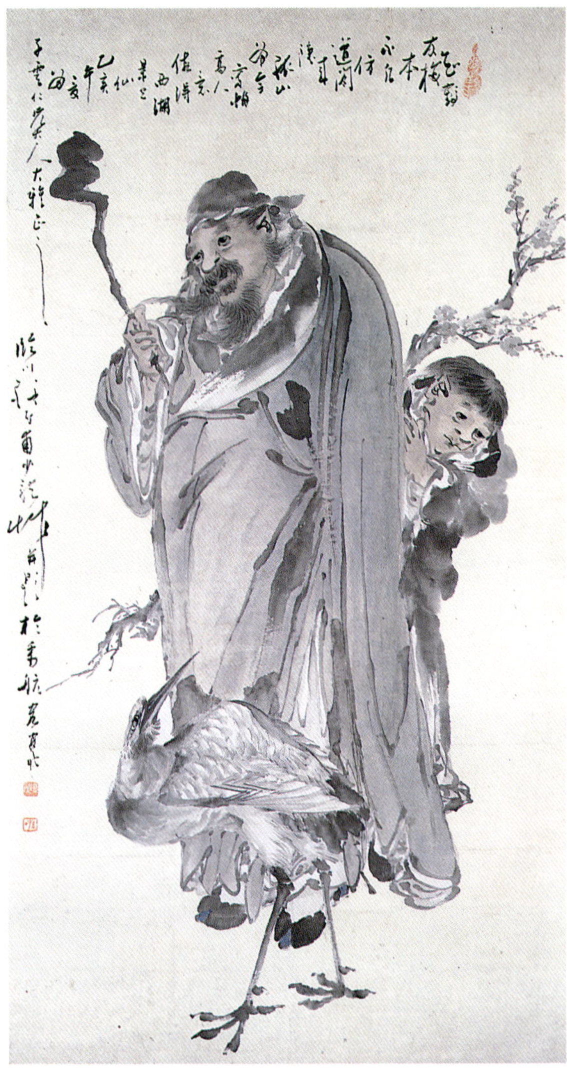

129

129 ARTIST UNKNOWN
Figure

INK AND SLIGHT COLOUR ON PAPER

HANGING SCROLL, 142 × 77 CM

EA 1995.248

Inscribed: 乙亥午夏爲子雲仁兄大人大雅正之
臨川 ＿ ＿ 甫少龍(?)草并題於 ＿ 航客 ＿ ＿
Painted for Mr. Ziyun in summer 1899 by Mr. _ _ of
Linchuan at _ while staying with _ _

Figure paintings, particularly those depicting
immortals or legendary heroes, were popular
subjects for commemorative or New Year pictures.
This work is not unsigned, but the calligraphy is
unclear and it is only possible to establish that the
artist was from Linchuan in Jiangxi province. The
extensive use of courtesy words suggests that it was
a valued commission.

130 ARTIST UNKNOWN
Tiger

INK AND COLOUR ON PAPER

HANGING SCROLL, 164 × 88 CM

EA 1995.249

Inscribed: 堯卿宗兄雅屬　爭之敬贈

This painting is in Lingnan School style. The artist
is unknown but one of the seals reads *Cai Xian*;
comparable works by the Lingnan master Gao
Qifeng suggest that Cai Xian may have been a pupil
of his, or perhaps an associate of one of his pupils.

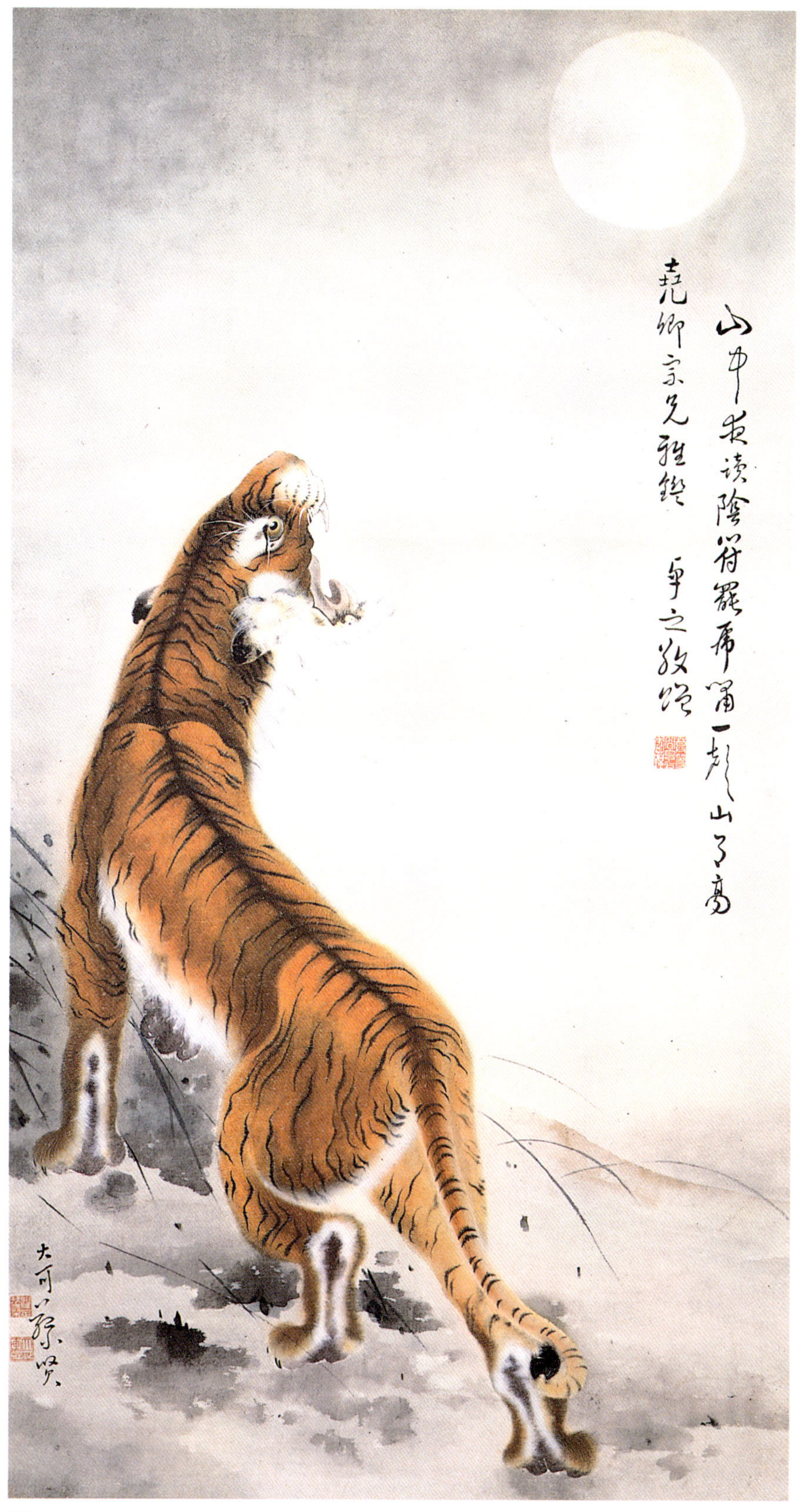

Andrews, Julia, *Painters and Politics in the People's Republic of China, 1949-1979*, Berkeley and Los Angeles, 1994.

Brown, Claudia and Chou Ju-Hsi, *Transcending Turmoil: Painting at the Close of China's Empire 1796–1911*, Phoenix, 1992.

Cahill, James, *Chinese Painting*, Geneva, 1977.

Cohen, Joan, *The New Chinese Painting, 1949-1986*, New York, 1987.

Hong Kong Museum of Art, *Twentieth Century Chinese Painting: Tradition and Innovation*, Hong Kong, 1995.

Hajek, Lubor, Adolf Hoffmeister and Eva Rychterova, *Contemporary Chinese Painting*, translated by Jean Layton, London, 1961.

Hejzlar, Josef, *Chinese Watercolours*, London, 1978.

Kao Mayching, ed., *Twentieth Century Chinese Painting*, Oxford, 1988.

Laing, Ellen Johnston, *The Winking Owl: Art in the People's Republic of China*, Berkeley and Los Angeles, 1988.

Li, Chu-tsing, *Trends in Modern Chinese Painting (The C.A. Drenowatz Collection)*, Artibus Asiae Supplementum 36, Ascona, 1979.

Silbergeld, Jerome, with Gong Jisui, *Contradictions: Artistic Life, the Socialist State, and the Chinese Painter Li Huasheng*, Seattle, 1993.

Sullivan, Michael, *Chinese Art in the Twentieth Century*, Berkeley, 1959.

Sullivan, Michael, *Art and Artists of Twentieth Century China*, Berkeley, 1996.